"My name is Patricia Rommel" ... investigations on murder cases for sen...

Pa...
of...

"Meyer died in Malawi and was buried at ... in Zomba." … "We attended his funeral."

Malawi Army Major to Author. 20 March, 2002

"Rommel had shown us his General Field Marshal uniform, revolver and medals including photos taken with Hitler and other photos."

Malawi Army Major to Author. March, 2002

"He married a black woman and frequented English Club in Zomba" … "He bought a caravan in Cape Town and travelled to Malawi."

Rudolf Hartwich, Newlands Home, Malawi 16 January, 2016

"There is a white person calling himself Meyer who has recently opened a lodge off Cholo Road, Limbe, Malawi."

John Lord talking on phone to John Weeks from Cape Town 19 January, 2016

"His full name is THUVAN PATRICK MEYER."

Manager at Lodge to John Weeks about Rommel's grandson 21 January 2016

"She also told me about my Grandfather being Rommel"

Shamim to Author on what her aunt Hendrina told her. 3 April 2017

GENERAL FIELD MARSHAL
ERWIN ROMMEL

MYTH OF HIS CREMATION IN GERMANY :
A SHOCKING REVELATION

Dr Tony Patel
&
John Stretton Weeks

Matador
9 Priory Business Park,
Wistow Road, Kibworth Beauchamp,
Leicestershire. LE8 0RX
Tel: 0116 279 2299
Email: books@troubador.co.uk
Web: www.troubador.co.uk/matador
Twitter: @matadorbooks

ISBN 978 1838590 369

British Library Cataloguing in Publication Data.
A catalogue record for this book is available from the British Library.

Printed and bound by CPI Group (UK) Ltd, Croydon, CR0 4YY
Typeset in 11pt Adobe Caslon Pro by Troubador Publishing Ltd, Leicester, UK

Matador is an imprint of Troubador Publishing Ltd

ABOUT THE AUTHORS

AUTHOR

Dr. Tony Patel was born in Limbe, Malawi on June 19, 1948. He was educated both in Malawi and England. He holds a BSc.(Hons) Arch. from North London Polytechnic (1978) and after returning back to Malawi in 1980, he obtained a PhD in History from Rutherford University, State of Wyoming, USA at the age of 57 years which was  marked by Late Prof. Noel King M.A. Oxon, PhD Nottingham, Prof. Klaus Fiedler PhD.; D. Theol (Heidelburg) and Dr. W.1.. Weston, PhD (California). Dr. Patel is a Historian/Researcher and has written books on the Sikh soldiers of the Raj who were brought to the British Colony here in Malawi (1881-1913 – PhD. dissertation), history of the earliest ancestors of the Irish at 1500 B.C., history of the establishment of a Indian State in Africa (c. 700 to B.C. 1330 A.D.) and history of the Arabs. He owns the largest private collection of Historical documents in his mini-museum including original letters written by Dr. David Livingstone, Sir Harry Johnstone, General Kleber (Napoleon's General in Egypt) and others.

John Stretton Weeks was born in Lewisham, England on October 30, 1945. He obtained a B.Sc. (Hons) degree in Geography from Southampton University in 1967 and a Dip. Ed. from Oxford University. Now retired in Malawi, after having taught Geography in Zambia for 15 years, he returned to England and  was Head of Geography at the British section of LYCEE FRANCAIS CHARLES DE GAULLE and taught here for 25 years. **Untill last year he has regularly travelled to England to conduct Juror services at Wood Green Crown Court.** His son is the chief security officer for EXON-MOBILE based in Brussels and his daughter-in-law was a former B.B.C. Foreign Correspondent and now an Activist with Human Rights Watch. She is the niece of Tony Hancock.

Contents

ACKNOWLEDGEMENTS

In gathering research material for this book, I have become indebted to so many people that it would be invidious to only mention a few. I would like to thank my co-author John who painstakingly researched and interviewed persons who had heard about Meyer alias Rommel being in Malawi. My thanks are also due to Rose Argente, Barrister-at-law, whose late father knew Rommel alias Meyer and in providing me with the most credible and compelling research evidence towards writing of this book.

Special thanks to Shamim, the grand-daughter of "Meyer" from his Malawian wife and to Thuvan, the grand-son of "Meyer" from his Afrikaner wife, both for providing information on them being Rommel's secret families .

Thanks are also due to Imran, a recent arrival into Malawi from India, to have typesetted the book's initial text, maps and photographs.

Dr. Tony Patel
Malawi, May 2019

FOREWORD

Books on the History of World War Two are plentiful. This book is not about the war with the Germans nor Hitler but that of the now standing controversy over Rommel's recorded death and **cremation** of that not being in Germany but his death and **burial** in the British protectorate of Nyasaland, now Republic of Malawi to where after 14th October 1944, he had escaped from Germany, not as the famous General, but under the false name of Meyer and left behind a secret family, first in South Africa and finally in Malawi.

Evidences presented in the foregoing chapters pointing to his death and burial being in Malawi are not just chance coincidences but have come about as a result of an astounding similarity of seven different (now connected) events recorded over a period of 21 years from reliable sources through correspondence and interviews with Rommel's friends, persons who had heard about him and family members, the most credible and compelling being the one provided by Rose Argente, Barrister-at-Law.

Also included is a chapter on a report made on 22nd July 1960 to Cologne Police by a Dr. Friedrich Brierderhoff that he was ordered by a S.S. man to falsify Rommel's death certificate and our methodical examination and arguments to disprove the authencity of his testimony.

Any record concerning Rommel's demise and final resting place which fails to take cognizance of, and give weight to, the evidences provided, will be so unrealistic that it should not be considered to have any value commanding consideration by serious and objective scholars, historians, film producers, governmental agencies and the like.

This book is then, aimed at two major audiences. Firstly, it is intended for the interested "Lay reader" and is secondly equally aimed at historians, politicians, concerned governments, documentary and film producers and other academics, in attempting to show that neither side of evidences provided consists of romantic fools or politically motivated knaves.

Proposals for the ultimate scientific evidence of Rommel's final resting place of that being in Malawi are presented in the book's conclusion.

Dr. Tony Patel
Author

John Stretton Weeks
Co-Author

CHAPTER ONE

About Erwin Rommel

INTRODUCTION

Below is presented a brief biography of Rommel and his campaigns at El Alamein in North Africa and some photographs and maps purely to provide a glimpse of his years as an officer of the army of the Third Reich.

ROMMEL, ERWIN (1891-1944). General field marshal, the famous Desert Fox of World War Erwin Rommel was born in Heidenheim, northeast of Ulm, on November 15, 1891. Entering the Army as a cadet in 1910, he became a professional soldier and devoted his life to that profession. He served in World War I as a lieutenant in an Alpine battalion in Romania and at Caporetto in Italy. In 1915 he was awarded the Iron Cross (First Class). After the war he remained in the Army as an infantry regimental officer and as an instructor at the Infantry School in Dresden. He met Hitler in 1935. In 1938, after reading Rommel's book *Infanterie greift an (Infantry Attacks),* Hitler appointed Rommel commander of his personal bodyguard battalion.

In World War II Rommel won a reputation as Germany's most popular general. At the same time he was regarded by many Allied officers as a master of desert warfare and as a fair-minded military professional. In 1940 he was assigned to command the 7th Panzer (Armored) Division on the western front under Gen. Gerd von Rundstedt. On February 6, 1941,

Hitler gave him command of the new Afrika Korps in North Africa with the task of pushing the British back into Egypt.

Rommel's campaign started successfully. On March 21, he defeated the British under Gen. Archibald Wavell at El Agheila and advanced to Tobruk. In late 1941 the British counterattacked and moved back to Benghazi. Rommel was promoted to full general in January 1942. On May 27, 1942, he struck swiftly in a renewed offensive and soon had the British reeling back toward the Egyptian frontier. On June 21, he captured Tobruk, the key to the British defenses. The next day Hitler made him a general field marshal. By the end of June 1942 Rommel was at El Alamein, 60 miles from Alexandria and the Nile Delta. It was one of the darkest moments of the war for the Allies.

Rommel's drive was halted by the end of October 1943 because of a combination of logistical difficulties and the buildup of Allied strength. Flown back to Germany for medical treatment, he returned to North Africa only after the Battle of El Alamein was lost (see EL ALAMEIN). Within two weeks he had to fall back 700 miles with the remnants of his African army. He was recalled from Tunis on March 9, 1943.

In mid-1943 Rommel was given command of Army Group B in northern Italy to prevent an Italian defection and to counter an Allied invasion of southern Europe. In January 1944 he was transferred to command of an army group in northern France. On two occasions, on June 17 and 29, 1944, Rommel and Von Rundstedt saw Hitler and attempted to convince him that he should end the war while considerable German forces still existed. The pale and shaken Fuehrer met their frankness with angry diatribes. On July 17, 1944, after the Allied invasion of Normandy, Rommel was severely injured when his Automobile was strafed by a British plane, and he was sent home to Ulm to recover.

By this time Rommel had become increasingly disillusioned not only by Hitler's unrealistic military leadership but also by the worldwide reaction to Nazi atrocities. The bluff, simple military man began to turn to politics. He opposed the projected assassination attempt on Hitler's life on the ground that this action would only create a martyr. He suggested that it was better to place the Fuehrer on trial to reveal his crimes to the nation.

Field Marshal Erwin Rommel

Rommel never took an active role in the July Plot, although the conspirators wanted him as Chief of State after the elimination of Hitler.

After the failure of the plot, one of the conspirators, before he died in agony on a meat hook, blurted out Rommel's name to his tormentors. Rommel's doom was sealed. The Fuehrer sent two officers to Rommel's home at Herrlingen bei Ulm on October 14, 1944, to give him the choice of suicide or trial. "I shall die in fifteen minutes," Rommel told his wife. He then took poison. Hitler ordered burial with full military honors. In his funeral oration Von Rundstedt said: "A pitiless destiny snatched him from us. His heart belonged to the Fuehrer[1].

EL ALAMEIN — ONE OF THE DECISIVE BATTLES OF WORLD WAR II.

On July 1, 1942, Gen. Erwin Rommel known as the Desert Fox, ordered his men of the Afrika Korps to stop at El Alamein, a stony, waterless desert spot about 60 miles west of Alexandria. Early the next month, Prime Minister Winston Churchill placed Gen. Bernard Law Montgomery in charge of the British Eighth Army. Throughout the summer, reinforcements—

jeeps, trucks, Sherman tanks, planes, and ammunition—were rushed to Montgomery from England and the United States. Montgomery waited to strike until he had superiority in armor and in the air. Reorganizing his army with extreme care, he used deception on a vast scale, convincing the Germans that he would strike in the south instead of in the north. **He spoke coldly to his troops: "Kill Germans, even the padres—one per weekday and two on Sundays."**

On October 23, 1942, Montgomery hurled his full strength against the Germans. First came a violent artillery attack. The whole horizon burst into tongues of flame: Then 41,000 troops, 9,000 vehicles of all kinds, and 1,000 tanks surged forward on the Afrika Korps. Australians, Englishmen, Scots, New Zealanders, and South Africans pushed forward. Rommel, at this time in Germany for medical attention, had drawn up defensive plans. At Hitler's urgent request he rushed back to North Africa by plane, only to find that the Battle of El Alamein was lost. When his counterattack failed, Rommel decided to withdraw on the night of November 2-3, 1942.

El Alamein was one of the great turning points of the war, a tremendous victory for the Allies and a disheartening defeat for Hitler. **"It may almost be said," commented Churchill, "before Alamein we never had a victory, after Alamein we never had a defeat."**[2]

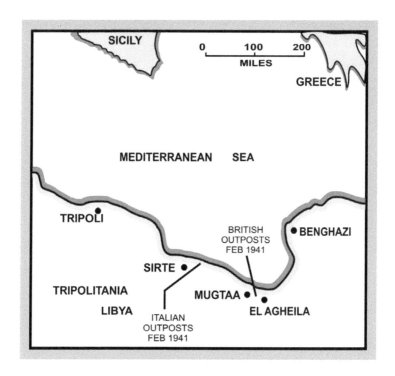

SOME MEMORABLE LETTERS WRITTEN BY ROMMEL
TO HIS WIFE FROM TRIPOLITANIA IN LIBYA

6 Feb. 1941

Dearest Lu,

Landed at Staaken 12.45. First to Ob.d.H. [C-in-C of the Army], who appointed me to my new job, and then to F. [Führer]. Things are moving fast. My kit is coming on here. I can only take barest necessities with me. Perhaps I'll be able to get the rest out soon. I need not tell you how my head is swimming with all the many things there are to be done. It'll be months before anything materialises.

So our leave' was cut short again. Don't be sad, it had to be. The new job is very big and important...

7 Feb. 1941

Slept on my new job last night. It's one way of getting my rheumatism treatment. [His wife was thus able to deduce that his new job was in Africa.] I've got a terrible lot to do, in the few hours that remain, getting together all I need.

14 Feb. 1941

Dearest Lu,

All going as well as I could wish. I hope to be able to pull it off. I'm very well. There's nothing whatever for you to worry about. A lot to do. I've already had a thorough look round.

17 Feb. 1941

Everything's splendid with me and mine in this glorious sunshine. I'm getting on very, very well with the Italian Command and couldn't wish for better co-operation.

My lads are already at the front, which has been moved about 350 miles to the east. As far as I am concerned they can come now.

26 March 1941

Dearest Lu,

Spent our first day by the sea. Its a very lovely place and its as good as being in a hotel in my comfortable caravan. Bathe in the sea in the mornings, its already beautifully warm. Aldinger and Gunther [Rommel's ADC and batman respectively] living in a tent close by. We make coffee in the mornings in our own kitchen. Yesterday an Italian general. Calvi de Bergolo, made me a present of a bournous. It's a magnificent thing – blue-black with red silk and embroidery. It would do well for you as a theatre cloak...

Little fresh from the front. I have to hold the troops back to prevent

*them bolting forward. They've taken another new position, 20
miles farther east. There'll be some worried faces among our Italian
friends.*

5 March 1941

Dearest Lu,

*Just back from a two-day journey— or rather flight —to the front,
which is now 450 miles away to the east. Everything going fine.*

*A lot to do. Can't leave here for the moment as I couldn't be
answerable for my absence. Too much depends on my own person
and my driving power. I hope you've had some post from me.*

*My troops are on their way. Speed is the one thing that matters
here. The climate suits me down to the ground. I even 'over-slept'
this morning till after 6…*

*A gala performance of Victory in the West [German
propaganda film of the 1940 French campaign] was given here
today. In welcoming the guests—there were a lot. some with
ladies —1 said I hoped the day would come when we'd be showing
Victory in Africa…*

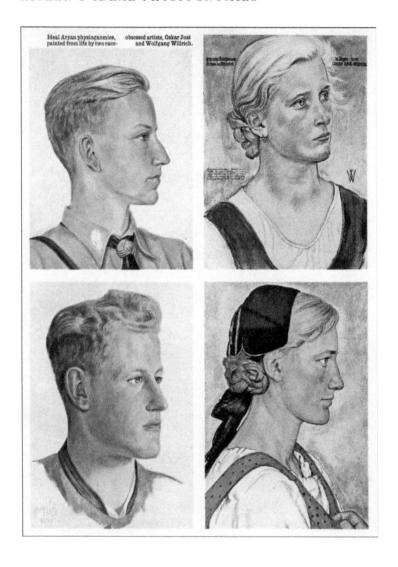

Ideal Aryan physiognomies, painted from life by two race-obsessed artists, Oskar Just and Wolfgang Willrich.

Weftifch   Nordifch

Dinarifch   Falifch

Oftifch   Oftbaltifch

How the racially impeccable Aryan was supposed to look: a chart of Teutonic types for classroom display, prepared by Dr Alfred Eydt. These categories, incidentally, are fictitious and unknown to physical anthropology : `Nordic', Falian' (as in Westfalian ), 'Eastern Baltic', `Western' (i.e. Rhinelanders, etc), `Dinaric' (such as might be found in Austria), and 'Eastern' (usually Germans of the Baltic regions).

Quoting from his biography[3], when Rommel's doom was sealed, Hitler sent two officers to his house at Herrlingen bei Ulm on October 14, 1944, to give him the choice of suicide or trial. Hitler put his plan in action, Rommel now noticed that his house was being shadowed by the S.D. When he went out walking in the nearby woods with his fifteen-year-old son, who had been given temporary leave from his antiaircraft battery to tend to his father, **both carried revolvers.** At headquarters in Rastenburg Hitler had now received a copy of Hofacker's testimony incriminating Rommel. He thereupon decreed his death—but in a special way. **The Fuehrer realized, as Keitel later explained to an interrogator at Nuremberg, "that it would be a terrible scandal in Germany if this well-known Field Marshal, the most popular general we had, were to be arrested and haled before the People's Court." So Hitler arranged with Keitel that Rommel would be told of the evidence against him and given the choice of killing himself or standing trial for treason before the People's Court. If he chose the first he would be given a state funeral with full military honors and his family would not be molested.**

Thus it was that at noon on October 14, 1944, two generals from Hitler's headquarters drove up to the Rommel home, which

was now surrounded by S.S. troops reinforced by five armored cars. The generals were Wilhelm Burgdorf, an alcoholic, florid-faced man who rivaled Keitel in his slavishness to Hitler, and his assistant in the Army Personnel Office, Ernst Maisel, of like character. **They had sent word ahead to Rommel that they were coming from Hitler to discuss his "next employment."**

"At the instigation of the Fuehrer," Keitel later testified, "I sent Burgdorf there with a copy of the testimony against Rommel. If it were true, he was to take the consequences. If it were not true, he would be exonerated by the court."

"And you instructed Burgdorf to take some poison with him, didn't you?" Keitel was asked.

"Yes. I told Burgdorf to take some poison along so that he could put it at Rommel's disposal, if conditions warranted it."

After Burgdorf and Maisel arrived it soon became evident that they had not come to discuss Rommel's next assignment. **They asked to talk with the Field Marshal alone and the three men retired to his study.**

"A few minutes later," Manfred Rommel later related, "I heard my father come upstairs and go into my mother's room." Then:

We went into my room. "I have just had to tell your mother," he began slowly, "that I shall be dead in a quarter of an hour . . . Hitler is charging me with high treason. In view of my services in Africa I am to have the chance of dying by poison. The two generals have brought it with them. It's fatal in three seconds. If I accept, none of the usual steps will be taken against my family . . . I'm to be given a state funeral. It's all been prepared to the last detail. In a quarter of an hour you will receive a call from the hospital in Ulm to say that I've had a brain seizure on the way to a conference."

And that is what (purportedly) happened.

Rommel, wearing his old Afrika Korps leather jacket **and grasping his field marshal's baton,** got into the car with the two generals, was driven a mile or two up the road by the side of a forest, where General Maisel and the S.S. driver got out, **leaving Rommel and General Burgdorf in the back seat.** When the two men returned to the car a minute later, Rommel was slumped over the seat, dead. **Burgdorf paced up and down impatiently, as though he feared he would be late for lunch and his midday drinks.** Fifteen minutes after she had bidden her husband farewell, Frau Rommel received the expected telephone call from the hospital. **The chief doctor reported that two generals had brought in the body of the Field Marshal, who had died of a cerebral embolism, apparently as the result of his previous skull fractures.** Actually Burgdorf had gruffly forbidden an autopsy. "Do not touch the corpse," he stormed. "Everything has already been arranged in Berlin." [8]

It had been.

(Authors' claim, Not everything "had been" as wrongly recorded.)

OUR REVELATIONS BEGIN HERE

Since it is known as a fact that many years after the end of the war, many infamous Nazis ,on account of their seniority and contacts, escaped to countries like Spain and South America , and apart from those who stood trial at Nuremburg, quite a handful who were hunted down and brought to Israel to stand trial for the horrendous atrocities they had committed on Jewish men, women and children under Hitlers 'final solution', there is no reason to disbelieve that Rommel being a General field marshal,[3] would have had direct contacts with senior military personnel and politicians in Italy, German East Africa and German Namibia who would have received him and provided him with a safe haven.

ROMMEL'S STATE FUNERAL WITH FULL MILITARY
HONOURS ARRANGED BY HITLER

Adolf Hitler (1889-1945)

Nuremburg Trial: The public trial of 22 German principals was held at Nuremburg from Nov. 1945 to Oct. 1946

Moreover, Rommel had ignored orders to kill Jewish soldiers, civilians and capture commandos, and was not accused of war crimes[54].

In a recent article[69], Rommel's son Manfred became an honorary "guardian of Jerusalem" on account of the fact that many north African Jews owed their lives to his father.

He however did not escape from Germany as Rommel, the famous General, but as an ordinary rich German civilian by the name of MEYER.

The world must know and ensure that this should never happen again

On May 9, 1945, one day
after being taken prisoner,
Hermann Goring[57] gave
a press conference in an
Augsburg garden. When
asked about his wartime
boast that if the Allies ever
bombed Berlin "My name
is MEYER", the usually
garrulous Goring reddened,
mopped his face and said
nothing.[58] One wonders
and it will still remain a

Hermann Goring

mystery as to why Goring called himself by this particular name
MEYER which Rommel had also called himself after escaping
from Germany just seven months earlier.

Before we reconstruct and unravel his plausible escape
routes out of Germany on or after October 14, 1944, the day of
his purported suicide, we will first examine the following two
records to deduce the sequence and timing of the event that
took place at Rommel's home at Herrlingen on 14th October,
1944 and then ask ourselves as to why he was never to return
back to his family at his home at Herrlingen bei Ulm.

RECORD NO. I

Statement by Captain Hermann Aldinger[60] dated October 13,
1944. Captain Hermann Aldinger on the day of Fieldmarshal
Erwin Rommel's death.

October 13, 1944

"On October 13th came a telephone call from headquarters of War District 5 at Stuttgart. Rommel and Aldinger were out and a soldier servant took the call. He was told to inform Fieldmarshal Rommel that General Burgdorf and General Maisel would arrive at Herrlingen next day at noon. When Rommel received the message he said very little. To Aldinger he remarked that the two generals were doubtless coming to talk to him about the invasion or about a new job. For the rest of the day he was unusually silent."

"At noon precisely General Burgdorf arrived with General Maisel and a Major Ehrenberger, another Ordonnanzoffizier. They came in a small green car. The driver wore a black uniform of the S.S. The two generals shook hands with Rommel. Frau (Mrs.) Rommel, Manfred, and Aldinger were introduced. After a moment General Burgdorf said that he wished to speak to the Fieldmarshal (Rommel) alone. Frau Rommel went upstairs to her room. Rommel led Burgdorf into a downstairs room and Maisel followed. As they moved away, Rommel turned to Aldinger to prepare his file of his orders and situation reports issued during the Normandy fighting, for he suspected that he was to be interrogated about the invasion. Aldinger's file was, of course, in order and he remained talking to Major Ehrenberger outside the front door while Manfred went upstairs to continue coloring some maps for his father. It was nearly an hour later that General Maisel came out. He was followed after a minute or two by General Burgdorf. Rommel was not with them. He had gone upstairs to his wife."

"As he was taking leave of his wife, Manfred entered the room cheerfully, to see what had become of his father. The generals were waiting for him. Rommel said good-bye to his son also. Then he turned and went into the room next door. Manfred followed at his heels. Rommel called for his soldier servant and sent him to find

Aldinger. To Aldinger he explained what was in store for him. He was now quite calm but Aldinger could hear Frau Rommel sobbing in her room. Aldinger was not disposed to take it like this. "I told him", he said, "that he must at least make an escape. Why could we not try to shoot our way out together?", asked Aldinger. 'We have been in as bad places before and got away." "It's not good, my friend", he said, "This is it! All the streets are blocked with S.S. cars and the Gestapo are all around the house. We could never get back to the troops. They've taken over the telephone. I cannot even ring up my headquarters." Aldinger said we could at least shoot Burgdorf and Maisel. "No", said Rommel, "they have their orders. I have Manfred and my wife to think of". Then he told me that he had been promised that no harm should come of them if he took the first choice. A pension would be paid. He was to be given a state funeral. **He would be buried at home in Herrlingen.** "I have spoken to my wife and made up my mind..", he said, "I will never allow myself to be hanged by that man, Hitler !! I planned no murder. I only tried to serve my country, as I have done all my life, but now this is what I must do. In about half an hour there will come a telephone call from Ulm to say that I have had an accident and am dead".

"Having taken his decision, Rommel went upstairs with Manfred and Aldinger. The generals were looking at the garden. They came over to the car and Rommel got in first into the back seat. Burgdorf and Maisel followed him. Major Ehrenberger had already left to make the arrangements."

"Twenty-five minutes later the telephone rang. Aldinger answered it. It was Major Ehrenberger, speaking from Ulm. "Aldinger", he said, "a terrible thing has happened, Fieldmarshal Rommel has had a hemmorhage, a brain storm, in the car!! He is dead!! "Aldinger did not reply. Did you hear what I said", asked Ehrenberger. "Yes", said Aldinger, "I heard." "Then please tell Frau (Mrs.) Rommel that I am coming back to the house at once." Aldinger walked slowly upstairs to Rommel's widow. He had no need to speak.

Authors' observation: The letter by Captain Aldinger was written on 13th October, 1944, the day **before** the event, means that he was with Rommel on this day. Most importantly, it would have been impossible for Aldinger to write of what happened on 14th October 1944 one day in advance!

RECORD NO. 2

Deposition[59] by Manfred Rommel dated 27 April, 1945.

From a combination of the below records, the following happened and what was to happen.

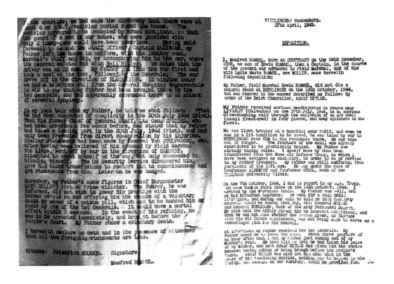

October 13, 1944: A telephone call came from the headquarters of War District 5 at Stuttgart. Rommel and Aldinger were out and a soldier servant took the call. He was told to inform Rommel that General Burgdorf[40] and General Maisel[41] would arrive at Herrlingen next day at noon. When Rommel received the message he said very little. To Aldinger he remarked that the two generals were doubtless coming to talk to him about the invasion or about a new job. For the rest of the day he was **unusually silent. (Note: The "unusual silence" was yet another indication of Rommel's confidence in his pre-arranged escape plan).**

(It may be worthwhile to note that it was Field Marshal Wilheim Keital[48] who had instructed Burgdorf to offer Rommel a choice — take poison, receive a state funeral, and obtain immunity for his family and staff, or face a trial for treason. In 1939, at the outbreak of World War II, Keital ranked No. 5 among the senior officers of the Army. On July 19, 1940 Keital was made a general field marshal, with eleven other generals, by a triumphant Hitler. However, it is remotely plausible that Rommel's pre-arranged escape could have been linked to Keital since his influence on Hitler had become increasingly limited as the war progressed **and moreover, he had threatened to resign in 1941 in order to discourage Hitler from invading the Soviet Union, but was unable to prevent the Fuehrer's invasion.** Keital was familiar with the Resistance movement against Hitler, but he vacillated from one side to the other. A non-Nazi rather than an anti-Nazi, he was by nature indecisive. Unfortunately for him, he relapsed with compliant obedience to Hitler and was found guilty at Nuremburg and executed on October 16, 1946).

It is our considered opinion that Keital being of the highest military rank, in his indecisive 'opportunity' could have had already secretly pre-arranged Rommel's escape through Burgdorf.

At this juncture it is clear that Aldinger[60] was with Rommel at Herrlingen. It is not known if Aldinger stayed the night at Rommel's home which he probably did or travelled to a nearby house and spent the night there. Earlier on, on the 7th October, 1944, according to Manfred, he had to report to his A.A. Troop and came back home on a short leave on the 14th October, 1944, which he did and arrived by the 6 o'clock train. He found his father in good health and they had breakfast together. Since Aldinger was not at the breakfast table, it is plausible that although he was with Rommel the previous day, he would have left Herrlingen late in the evening and would have stayed somewhere not far from Herrlingen where he would have woken up late in the morning, had breakfast, and arrived back at Herrlingen just before noon the next day. Anyhow, both Manfred and Rommel went out for a walk until 11 o'clock where Manfred was informed about the arrival of the two generals. Rommel also informed Manfred that "the affair struck him as somewhat suspicious, and that he was not sure whether the reason given, to discuss with him his future appointment, was not being made to serve as a camouflaged plot for his removal."

It is pertinent to note that when Manfred had gone for a walk with his father, they were both carrying revolvers.[4] (On Rommel's revolver: See Chapter 4 POINT C).

October 14, 1944: At noon precisely Burgdorf[40] and Maisel[41] and a Major Ehrenberger[61] drove up to Rommel's home in a small green car (Opel) driven by a S.S. driver (Master Sergeant Heinrich Doose) in black uniform. The two generals shook hands with Rommel. (It is doubtful and unusual that the two generals actually "shook hands" with Rommel. Being a General Field Marshal and much more senior in rank, one would have thought that the two generals would have approached him with the usual "Heil Hitler" salute which, of course, would have been reciprocated by Rommel in a similar way – this is attested by Manfred in his Deposition[59]).

Photo of open top Opel green color (1942-44)

By this time, according to Manfred , both him and his father had made the discovery that there were at least 4 or 5 M.T. vehicles posted round the house and the vehicles appeared to be occupied by armed civilians and that the guard of 8 men in the house who were provided with only 2 tommy – **guns would have been powerless.**

After "shaking hands" with Rommel, Mrs. Rommel, Manfred and Aldinger were introduced. **After a moment Burgdorf said that he wished to speak to Rommel alone.** Mrs. Rommel went upstairs to her room. Rommel then led Burgdorf into a downstairs room (his study) followed by Maisel and left them there. He then turned to Aldinger to prepare his file of his orders and situation reports issued during the Normandy fighting, for he suspected that he was to be interrogated about the invasion. Aldinger's file was, of course, in order and he remained talking to Major Ehrenberger outside the front door while Manfed went upstairs to continue coloring some maps for his father.

At this juncture, according to Manfred, in his last talk with his father **(and it is not known when this happened)** he was told, "That he had been suspected of complicity in the 20th July 1994 (Plot). That his former Chief of general Staff, Lt. Gen. SPEIDEL[36], who had been arrested a few weeks before, had stated that Rommel had taken a leading part in the Plot, and had only been prevented from direct co-operation by his injuries." **Most importantly, Manfred also stated that his father's name appeared in Chief Burgomaster GOER DELLE's LIST[62] as Prime Minister** (much to the outrage of Hitler who, not wishing to lower his prestige with the German people, was offering him the chance of a voluntary death by means of a poison pill, which was to be handed to him en route by one of the two Generals. It is important to note that although Rommel, on account of him being secretely informed in advance of what was in store for him (ie, the choice of "taking poison" or "stand trial for treason") by

General Spiedel36, his former Chief of Staff on 4th September, 1944 (some 6 weeks earlier) the day after he had visited him at Herrlingen[6], Manfred would not have known about the offer of the choices until after the message was conveyed to him by his father on 14th October, 1944.

This therefore means that Manfred did not tell the truth about "his last talk" with his father in his DEPOSITION made (some 6 months later) on 27th April, 1945 under a "declared OATH". It is doubtful that he would have had an access to the account of the event as recorded by Aldinger. After all, he was only 15 years old and simply recalled and/or reconstructed the "jumbled" events leading up to his Deposition which he made primarily to protect himself (advised possibly by Friedrich HUOBER[63], his witness) for any possible "future shape of things to come" pertaining to him being implicated with Hitler's Nazi Regime and indeed to clear his dad's name.

For the purpose of noting the sequence and the authencity of events in this book, it is really not important to debate on the "truthfulness" or otherwise of Manfred's DEPOSITION save to accept and note what he actually saw happening on October 14, 1944.

We now return to the sequence of events that took place. Rommel entered his study and was informed on his "next assignment" (the choice of taking poison) the cyanide capsule in Burgdorf's possession, or face being arrested to stand trial.

In our opinion, since Rommel had pre-planned his escape long before 14th October, 1944 for the reasons given in the following sections, he purportedly chose or at this juncture "agreed" to take poison. This being his "final moments", he would have been allowed to pour a drink and raise a toast to Hitler. This being "so", he also poured "stiff" drinks and offered them to both the generals, who he knew to be habitual alcoholics, gladly accepted. In the ¾ hour when all three were in the study there is no reason to disbelieve that drink after drink were poured, where on one hand Rommel simply filled his glass and kept throwing his drinks say, in a flower pot unnoticed and kept filling the glasses of the generals on the other hand so much so that both would have been "fairly" intoxicated by the time the two Generals walked out of the front door towards the car parked outside with the S.S. driver waiting by its side.

Rommel then went upstairs to say goodbye to his wife and conveyed the message which Manfred later related, "I heard my father come upstairs and go into my mother's room." Then: we went into my room "I just have to tell your mother ," he began slowly, "that I shall be dead in a quarter of an hour…Hitler is charging me with high treason. In view of my services in Africa I am to have the chance of dying by poison. The two generals have brought it with them. It's fatal in three seconds. If I accept, none of the usual steps will be taken against my family…I'm to be given a state funeral. It's all been prepared to the last detail. In a quarter of an hour you will receive a call from the hospital in Ulm to say that I've had a brain seizure on the way to a conference.[64]

Now, while the two generals were waiting outside for Rommel to join them, he said good-bye to his son also. He then turned and went into the room next door. Manfred followed at his heels. Rommel then called for his soldier servant and sent him to find Aldinger to whom he then explained what was in store for him. He was now quite calm (this calmness was the first sign of his confidence that his escape plan was imminent and guaranteed) but Aldinger could hear Mrs. Rommel sobbing in her room. Aldinger was not disposed to take it like this. "I told him" he said, "that he must at least make and escape. Why could we not try to shoot our way out together?", asked Aldinger, "we have been in as bad places before and got away". "It's not good, my friend", Rommel said, "This is it! All the streets are blocked with S.S. cars and the Gestapo are all round the house. We could never get back to the troops. They've taken over the telephone. I cannot even ring up my headquarters. Here again, in our opinion, although Rommel was right about the house being surrounded by the Gestapo, it would'nt have been possible when he mentioned of the telephone being taken over and his failure to ring up his headquarters. He could have only tried to use the phone in his study when the two generals were present which would have been impossible. This again points to his confidence of his planned escape and even if he admired the loyalty of Aldinger, which he did, he simply informed him that his proposals to shoot their way out were not "workable".

*Loyalty: Captain Aldinger (a landscape architect in civilian life) had been on friendly terms with Rommel eversince the First World War. He had already accompanied Rommel in 1940 in France and in 1941 he was Rommel's ADC and lived in a tent close by Rommel's tent at El Agheila, the British Fort, water points, and airfield which Rommel's Battalion took on March 24, 1941.

Furthermore, when Aldinger suggested that they could at least shoot Burgdorf and Maisel, Rommel had replied, "they have their orders. I have Manfred and my wife to think of". Yet again Rommel only replied to Aldinger and provided this reasoning lest his escape plans would be foiled. Continuing, just before the generals had arrived at his house, both Rommel and his 15 year old son were carrying revolvers as mentioned earlier[4].

Although Rommel was allowed to wear his old Africa Korps leather jacket and take his Field Marshal's baton there is no record that his revolver was stripped off of him **before** and **after** he sat in the back seat of the car with Burgdorf. (Rommel's revolver: see Chapter 4 Point C.)

Note: In another version[71] of the conversation between Rommel and his son Manfred, Rommel had said SARCASTICALLY, "I am to have the chance of dying by poison". In our opinion, this SARCASM was yet another reason that Rommel was confident that his pre-arranged faked death and escape from Germany was guaranteed. Manfred also stated that, "It was not then ENTIRELY CLEAR, what happened to him after he left us". This also suggests that the telephone call received by Manfred from General Hospital Wagnerschule was pre-arranged and a fake one.

By the time Rommel said farewell to his family and Aldinger and sat in the open top car, it would have been 1:15 pm. He was then driven a mile or two up the road by the side of a forest in the direction of BLAUBEUREN. This would have been around 1:30 pm.

At this juncture, according to MANFRED "15 minutes later we had a telephone call from the General Hospital Wagnerschule in Ulm to say that my father had been brought there by the two Generals, and had apparently succumbed there to an attack of cerebral apoplexy". **Unless this was pre-planned,** it would have been impossible for Manfred to have received the telephone call "15 minutes later", ie at 1:15 pm from the hospital simply because this was the time when there were only Burgdorf and Rommel in the back seat of the car at the spot by the side of the forest at around 1:30 pm.

The only possible and plausible explanation for the call to Manfred from the hospital, which he no doubt received, is that it must have been pre-planned to this detail by Burgdorf's contacts at the hospital / Stuttgart / Berlin who had knowledge in advance of what Hitler had in mind (ie, his plan to send the two generals and inform Rommel on the choice of taking poison or stand trial).

To sum up, it would have been impossible for Manfred to have received the telephone call 15 minutes later, ie at 1:15 pm from the hospital simply because, firstly, this was the time when there was only Burgdorf and Rommel in the back seat of the car at the spot by the side of the forest at around 1:30 pm and secondly, assuming that ten minutes[71] after Maisel and the driver had returned to the car and Rommel lay "dead" slumped in the back seat and driven to the hospital which was about 10.5 kilometers away from the spot of his "alleged" suicide, the car would have arrived at the hospital at around 2:15 pm.

We now return to the scene in the back seat of the car. We only had Burgdorf and Rommel, who was armed. This is not to suggest that Rommel got his revolver out and forced him to summon Maisel and the S.S. driver back into the car (who had returned to the car ten minutes later) but this could have been a possibility where they could have been ordered to drive a few miles further to a secret location where his contacts were in wait for his pre-planned escape.

However, what would be more possible and plausible is that after giving the generals stiff drinks in his study who would have been craving for more [(both of whom were scared of Hitler on one hand, and also of Rommel, whom they were aware would

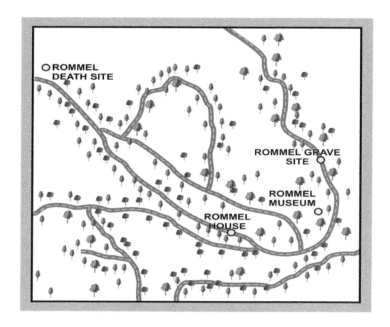

be the leader of Germany and would eventually be their boss) after Hitler's assassination], he would have instructed Burgdorf to have him driven to the secret location and return back to "do the needful" which he did. (See "Faked Evidence" on page 38).

It is important to note that Maisel was not present when Burgdof offered Rommel with a cyanide capsule. While he accompanied Burgdof in escorting Rommel in the vehicle driven by the S.S. driver to the location where Rommel was to take the cyanide capsule and after returning to the hospital, Maisel was once again dismissed by Burgdorf, thus only saw Rommel's "remains" but did not witness the process.[30] (In our opinion, even this is doubtful: Apart from this statement cited by the Author[30], there is no official record of Maisel having seen the "remains" ie, "ashes").

Moreover, when the two generals had brought in the "body" of Rommel, General Burgdorf had gruffly forbidden an autopsy and had stormed, "don't touch the corpse"… "Everything has been arranged in Berlin".

The question which now arises is as to why the pathologist was not allowed to touch the corpse to conduct an autopsy?

Apart from the propaganda arrangements later made in Berlin regarding Rommel's demise due to an attack of cerebral apoplexy, we are of the considered opinion that **it was Rommel himself and General Burgdorf (possibly assisted earlier in the "plan" by Major Ehrenberger[61]) who faked his death before his escape from the forest was facilitated,** a plan that was pre-arranged by Rommel in Berlin and by those who wished that he would return as their leader after Hitler's assassination.

WILHELM BURGDORF

As it so happened, it timeously worked out well for Rommel (who escaped from Germany) and the two generals after all, except for Rommel, could not have been of Hitler's list of conspirators since they had loyally followed his "instructions."

As for Burgdorf, following the earlier suicide by Hitler and Goebbels, he and his colleague Chief of Staff Hans Krebs[56] committed suicide by gun shots to the head on 2 May 1945.

As for Maisel, he was captured by the Americans on 7 May 1945 and was imprisoned until May 1947. He died on 16 Dec 1978 in Bavaria, Germany.

PLAUSIBLE ESCAPE ROUTES

At 1.30 pm, there were only Burgdorf and Rommel in the back seat of the car. In our reconstruction of what happened next (see "Faked Evidence" below), Burgdorf first ordered Maisel and the S.S. driver to walk away towards Herrlingen in the forest where he ensured that both could not see what was to happen. As soon as they were out of sight, Rommel got out of the car, walked about 10 metres, and sat in another unmarked car pre-arranged by him to be parked unseen behind trees in the forest. **At this juncture, the question arises as to how he had communicated 11/2 hours earlier from his study to those who had agreed to his escape plan on this particular day. The answer is that he must have somehow managed to communicate from a phone when Burgdorf and Maissel left his study which fits in with his master plan pre-arranged to this detail based on the choice of options conveyed to him by General Speidel on 4th September 1944, the day after he had visited him at his house in Herrlingen. (and that is why he was calm all through the day in question).**

Returning to the scene in the forest: Just after Rommel sat in the car mentioned, simultaneously another car driven by somebody posing as S.S. driver drove up to where Burgdorf was standing and he got into it. This exercise was completed in 6 minutes. After about 10 minutes, Maisel and the S.S. driver arrived at the spot where Burgdorf informed Maisel that Rommel had taken the cyanide capsule (he did'nt have to tell him this) and that he personally dumped his body in the forest nearby and would wait to "take photographs". He would have lied to Maisel that the car he sat in had already been arranged for him from Berlin.

He then ordered Maisel and the S.S. driver to drive back to General Hospital Wagnerschule and wait there for him or drive to a restaurant/bar where Maisel could have his lunch or continue drinking or even go home.

When the "coast was clear", Burgdorf got driven where Rommel waited for the faked film of him taken shown "dead", an exercise that was completed in about 15 minutes (actually it did not now matter how long this took). Burgdorf collected the movie camera and got driven to a photographic studio and had the film roll processed for him to "do the needful" pertaining to his task of sorting out the issue of funeral ceremony, photos for Hitler, cremation etc. He had 3 clear days to do this exercise.

Meanwhile, after the film of "dead" Rommel was taken, Rommel was driven to a "barn" or "bunker" from where his pre-arranged forged documents, substantial cash (or even gold bars), luggage typed and labelled with the name MEYER, were ready for him.

THE FAKED EVIDENCE

It is our considered opinion that the whole issue of evidence based on film of Rommel's demise hinged on the master fakery which Rommel himself had pre-arranged with Burgdorf and a cameraman (or Burgdorf with a movie camera) who took and shot the film shown below in which Rommel (still alive) is portrayed as being dead with his full military uniform, the film being shot to show Hitler and the German people that he had "succumbed to an attack of cerebral apoplexy" and died.

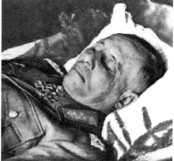

If the above photographs from the film are examined closely, the following will be noticed followed by what ought to have happened, what did not happen and what actually happened.

a. That they are taken in the open where there are trees in the background which can only be in the forest where General Burgdorf had allegedly given Rommel the cyanide capsule.

b. That he is laid on a stretcher and not in a coffin befitting a General Field Marshal.

c. That he is not laid in an open coffin in the church near his house in Herrlingen (or a Military Hall) attended by a priest where his family, relatives, friends and senior military officers could view his body and pay their last respects/ tributes.

d. That prior to the film being shot, Rommel wore his uniform (linked up in chapter 4 and 5), lay on the stretcher with his head resting on a pillow and closed his eyes, after which the film was shot, a pre-arranged exercise which could not have taken more than 15 minutes.

e. That the whole idea of cremation (unless ofcourse pre-planned to detail by Rommel himself) somehow does not make sense (there is no record that his wife or son Manfred had requested his cremation) in that Rommel was raised strictly as a Protestant, having being baptized on the second day of his birth on 15th November, 1891, he would have been buried in a coffin. Moreover, apart from the mass "cremations" of Jews and others in the furnaces of the concentration camps, no crematorium in Germany existed in or before 1944 particularly in the vicinity of Herrlingen or the hospital where the "body" was taken.

f. That when the "body" was taken to General Hospital Wagnerschule, General Burgdorf had ordered the doctor/pathologist not to touch the corpse. This strict order meant that it was not Rommel's body and since nobody saw it, a corpse of somebody or a dummy would have had to have been placed in order to conceal what happened at the scene of the alleged suicide.

g. That when the swastika bedecked coffin was paraded at the full Military honours ceremony, the pall bearers were carrying a coffin which, to avoid suspicions on the weight, an object (eg. body of some other person, plentiful to have been collected from the mortuary or even a log) was placed in it.

h. That when the "corpse" was burnt, nobody except for Burgdorf saw it before the ashes were placed in an Urn which was presented to Rommel's wife and son.

i. That on the sole evidence of the film shot of the "dead" Rommel, Hitler was convinced beyond any shadow of doubt that his offer to Rommel of one of the choices (ie. committing suicide) was carried out by Burgdorf through instructions from Field Marshal Wilhelm Keital. Rommel's master fakery was pre-arranged just for this Purpose...convincing Hitler of his death and escaping out of Germany.

j. That Rommel's funeral procession took place on 18th October, 1944 four days after he had allegedly committed suicide. Assuming that his "body" was kept in a mortuary, apart from being seen by Burgdorf only, there is no record of where it was kept suggesting that the "corpse" was not in a "cold-room". The unattended four day period was quite a task for Burgdorf to have hidden the "corpse" to avoid it being opened by any medical staff.

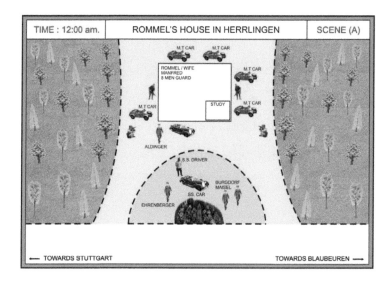

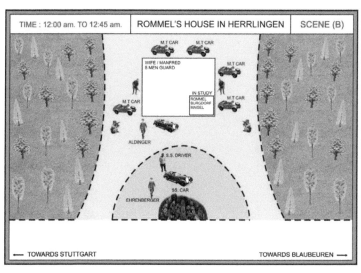

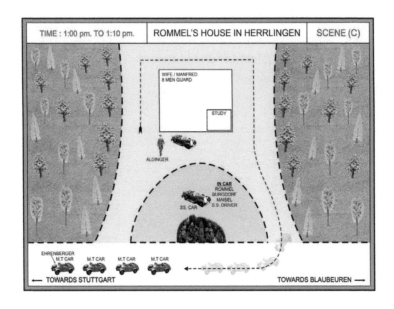

TIME : 1:00 pm. TO 1:10 pm. | ROMMEL'S HOUSE IN HERRLINGEN | SCENE (C)

WIFE / MANFRED
8 MEN GUARD

STUDY

ALDINGER

IN CAR
ROMMEL
BURGDORF
MAISEL
S.S. DRIVER

S.S. CAR

EHRENBERGER
M.T CAR   M.T CAR   M.T CAR   M.T CAR

← TOWARDS STUTTGART   TOWARDS BLAUBEUREN →

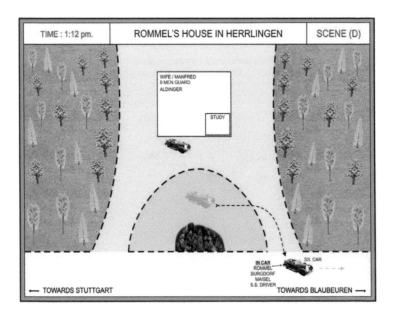

TIME : 1:12 pm. | ROMMEL'S HOUSE IN HERRLINGEN | SCENE (D)

WIFE / MANFRED
8 MEN GUARD
ALDINGER

STUDY

IN CAR
ROMMEL
BURGDORF
MAISEL
S.S. DRIVER

S.S. CAR

← TOWARDS STUTTGART   TOWARDS BLAUBEUREN →

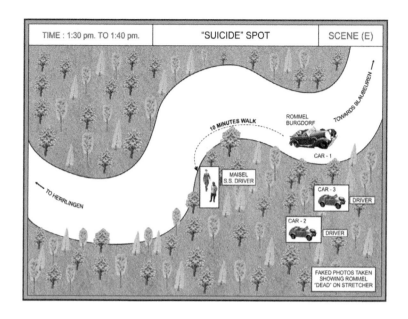

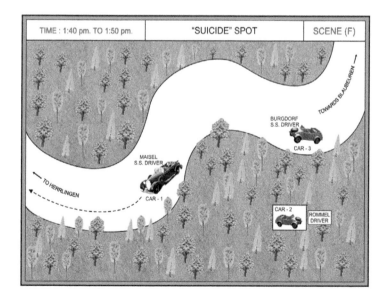

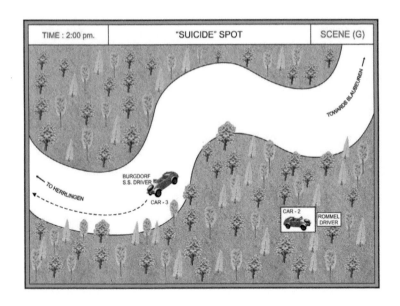

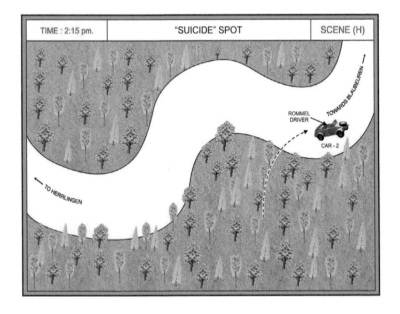

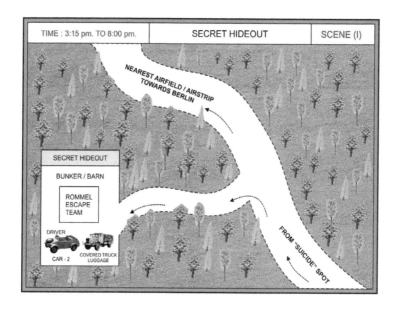

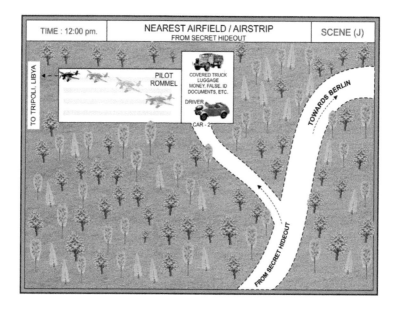

Aircraft similar to the one above in which Rommel would have been flown.

FAKED DEATH RECONTRUCTION – SEQUENCE OF EVENTS

From this "barn" or "bunker", under cover of darkness, he would have been driven to a remote airfield or airstrip and unlike Rudolf Hess who flew solo to Scotland earlier on May 10, 1941, he would have been flown in a small two seater seaplane or other aircraft (possibly by Lieut. Col. Wolfgang Schenk of the German Luftwaffe. Wolfgang was born in Windhoek, Namibia) to North Africa **(six months before the execution of Mussolini,**[49] **when Italians were still allies of the Germans)** which would have landed at a coast near Tripoli in Libya and he would have, under disguise of an Arab businessman with forged identity documents under an Arabic name or even as a German businessman by the name Meyer, been received.

Here, within days, his Italian contacts would have facilitated a passenger plane which would have flown him to Mombasa airport in German East Africa. From here he would have been flown to Windhoek Airport in German Namibia.

In Namibia, even if he did not use his contacts, he would have simply been cleared by the immigration officials wearing a hat, dark glasses, false moustache and carrying his luggage/ trunks under the name Meyer, a rich German

Plausible Arab disguise.

businessman. This would have been at the end of October, 1944 when he was only 53 years old.

Plausible businessman disguise

He would have had sufficient funds to reside in Namibia from October 1944 to 1945. To avoid being recognized and to be extra careful, he would have rented a house on the remote shores of Walvis Bay, the Skeleton Coast.

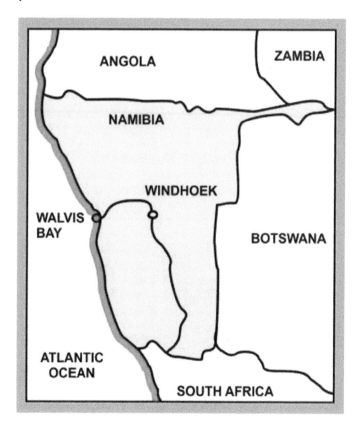

Left: Hellmut in Germany 1941
Middle: Hellmut with Rommel in North Africa 1942
Right: Hellmut with his wife in Namibia c. 2014

However, having arrived in Namibia, it is more than likely that he contacted **Hellmut von Leipzig** (who was born on 18th July, 1921 in Keetmanshoop, Namibia and died on 24th October 2016, Namibia and who was his driver in his North African Campaigns) **to have driven him around and carrying out other errands for him.**

His short stay in Namibia would have been due to the extremely hot and harsh weather conditions of the Namib Desert.

He would have then arrived back to Windhoek and taken a train or plane here to arrive at Johannesburg in South Africa and befriended Germans (possibly through contacts provided by Hellmut) particularly those residing in Pretoria. **Among the Germans born in South Africa who served Hitler** (For eg. Robey Liebbrandt, born in Potchestroom, Western Transvaal, a spy and

Left: Heinz Schmidt with Rommel in North Africa 1942
Right: Heinz Schmidt in Johannesburg in his retirement years

saboteur and Wilhelm Joswig, born in Johannesburg, fighter pilot in German Luftwaffe) **Rommel would have contacted Heinz Werner Schmidt who had joined his staff in March 1941 from Eritrea and was his aide-de-camp and advisor.**

Heinz Schmidt would have advised Rommel to contact a plastic surgeon to carry out surgery on his nose in c. 1946 (see chapter 4 POINT E).

Even today, there are quite a handful who keep Hitler's portrait and Nazi paraphenalia in their houses and still have an admiration for Rommel[51]. **He would have stayed in South Africa upto the end of 1948. Here he "married" a European (Afrikaaner) lady and had children by the name of Patrick and Patricia (See chapter Eleven).**

He would have been 57 years old when he married the European leady.

From here, he travelled to Cape Town either by train or plane where he bought a caravan (see chapter 4, 6, 7) and eventually arrived into British Nyasaland under the name Meyer in C. 1949. He would have been 58 years old. He then "married"[67] a local 'black' woman by the name of Grace who was 22 years his junior (see chapter 5). Grace would have been born in 1914 and was 35 years old when she married Meyer.

Caravan similar to the one purchased by Rommel.

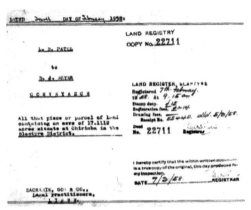

Dr. D. M. Patel
(1907-1978)

He first stayed in the caravan (purchased in Cape Town) parked on a plot just before entering Zomba (the then capital of the country) and frequented Zomba Gymkhana Club (see chapter 4 and Chapter 6). This would have been from 1949 to 1952.

He then moved to Chirimba in C. 1953 and was a friend/ neighbor of Rose Argente's father to whom he had revealed in confidence that he was indeed Rommel, (see chapter 5). He would have been 62 years old. He had first rented a house across the road to Chileka Airport from where Rose's family lived.

The Author's father (being a land surveyor qualified in India in 1927), between 1942 and 1960, owned large parcels of land in Malawi including some 17 Acres which he had sold to D.J. Meyer on behalf of his daughter L.B. Patel on 9th February 1958.

Meyer had twins by the name of Patricia (see chapter 3,4,5,8) and Patrick (see chapter 5) and three other daughters.

When the author's nephew got murdered on 6th January 1998, Patricia, who called herself Patricia Rommel (see chapter 3) and her brother Patrick Meyer (see chapter 12) would have been 43 years old. They therefore would have been born in Malawi in C.1955. This means that Rommel was about 64 years old when his wife Grace gave them birth.

a. In reconstructing his escape from Germany, he would have pre-planned it before 14th October, 1944 when he was receiving medical treatment "for bad fractures on his skull, temples and cheekbones and a severe injury to his left eye, his head being pitted with shell fragments which were first removed from a field hospital at Bernay to St. Germain to escape capture by the advancing Allied troops and thence on August 8, 1942 to his home at Herrlingen near Ulm."[4]

b. He would already have had false identity documents prepared for him calling himself MEYER just like the following example5 of a forged document of a prisoner held by the Germans or similar to the one shown.[66]

c. He had already received the first warning of what might be in store for him from General Spediel[36], his former Chief of Staff. This happened on September 4, 1944, the day after he had visited him at Herrlingen[6].

d. Under hideous tortures by the Gestapo, Colonel von Hofacker[38] had implicated Rommel in the conspiracy to assassinate Hitler. "Tell the people in Berlin they can count on me", Hofacker quoted Rommel as assuring him. It was a phrase that stuck in Hitler's mind when he heard of it and which led him to decide that his favorite general, whom he knew to be the most popular one in Germany, must die[7]. **Rommel would have been aware of Hitler's threat and had a reason to escape from Germany.**

FURTHER PLAUSIBLE REASONS FOR ROMMEL NOT RETURNING BACK TO GERMANY

a. Even though he would not have been directly responsible for the horrendous atrocities carried out by the Nazis on the Jews and others, he did command operations in France/ Belgium where thousands died. He therefore feared of being tried and being imprisoned at Nuremberg and the French, Belgians and Russians would have been on the fore front to ensure this. **On account of the consideration that many allied officers regarded him as a fair – minded military professional, the least he would have had to accept was imprisonment, which he was not keen to endure.**

b. When he allegedly took poison, he qualified for a funeral with full military honours and a message of gratitude from Hitler: **"His name has entered the history of the German 'Volk".** And though Hitler told the Germans that the attempted assassination had been a work of a small clique, the Getsapo arrested and killed nearly five thousand people in connection with it[10]. **He most certainly would have been shot, a reason for not returning back to Germany.**

c. When trapped in Tunisia with his Africa Korps, Hitler had ordered, "show your troops no other way expect to victory or death" a course which he was careful to avoid.

   This inaction by him would have been known by the Getsapo. Reason for him to escape from Germany.

d. As early December 1943, the Russians had began trying and executing German war criminals they had captured on their counter – offensive.[12] **He would have been aware of this and feared his fate at the hands of the Russians.**

e. On 14th November 1943, Dr Goebbels[42] wrote in 'Das Reich': **"So far as concerns us, we have burnt our bridges behind us. We can no longer turn back, nor do we want to turn back. We shall go down in history as the greatest statesmen of all time, or as its greatest criminals."[13] Rommel would have read this and would have feared as being classed a criminal and feared being tried at Nuremburg.**

f. On 6th June 1944, when Hitler received word that the Allies had landed in Normandy, he declared; **"The news couldn't be better! As long as they were in England we couldn't get at them. Now at last we have them where we can beat them".**[14]

   What he now expected of all Germans, both soldiers and civilians was that they should 'stand firm in the face of the impossible.' If they did not do this, he preferred to have them shot, as was the case of the five army officers who were executed by a 'flying court-marshal' for failing to blow up the Rhine Bridge Remagen in time to keep it from falling into American hands.

Here again, Rommel would have known of the executions and would have been implicated for his failures in North Africa and would have been subjected to such executions by a 'flying court-martial', yet another reason for escaping Germany.

g. In May 1940, Rommel's division had spearheaded the German advance through Belgium into France.[15] The devastation caused by his tanks to buildings which killed thousands of innocent men, women and children were his sole responsibility of "an infantryman turned tank General".[16] He feared being tried at Nuremburg for these acts of crimes against humanity and did not return to Germany.

h. On October 4, 1943. Hitler instructed Kesserling[17] to make a stand on a line across Italy between Naples and Rome and by 9th October, Hitler was speaking of "the decisive importance" of the line and had ordered Rommel in the north to send Kesserling two infantry divisions and some artillery. The Germans would hold south of Rome, Kesserling would command all German troops in Italy; and Rommel who had disapproved totally of this development, was to be sent to France to prepare against Allied invasion of Normandy.[18]

Rommel had essentially gone against Hitler's orders and had attempted to avoid assistance to Kesserling who cared little for Hitler and who did not wish him a particularly long life. He merely crouched his orders in an acceptable form, knowing that they would be read in Berlin.[19] Kesserling was later tried and condemned to his death for his involvement at Grotte Via Ardeatina, a cave near Rome where 330 Italian civilians were machine gunned to death on March 24, 1944.[20]

Yet again, Rommel knew that he could have been implicated indirectly with Kesserling's action and feared death (by Getsapo) or life imprisonment from British Court-Martial had he not escaped from Germany.

i. On 17 June 1944, Hitler himself had put in a brief appearance and had held a conference at Margival near Soissans. He had demanded explanations from Von Rundstedt21 and Rommel, and he had received from the latter a forthright assessment of Allied strength which provoked an outburst from Hitler, **"Don't you worry about the future course of the war. Stick to your own invasion front."**[22]

    Rommel was aware of Hitler's outburst and knew that he had to escape from Germany.

j. When Hitler survived a plot to assassinate him on 20 July 1944, it was his wish that the plotters "be hanged like cattle." The leaders of the plot had included Colonel-General Ludwig Beck23 and Serving officers like General Von Stulpnagel.24 Von Kluge25 and Rommel were both to some extent implicated.26

    Rommel was aware that he was on the plotter's list and had to escape from Germany.

k. When on May 14, 1940 once over the Meuse River, (on the France-Belgium border) Rommel who had taken his 7th Panzer Division and spread terror in the French rear, described the carnage his tanks had inflicted on them: "… **Civilians and French troops, their faces distorted with terror, lay huddled in the ditches, alongside hedges and in every hollow beside the road…Always the same picture, troops and civilians in wild flight down both sides of the road…a chaos of guns, tanks and military vehicles of all kinds, inextricably with horse-drawn refuge carts."**[27] Rommel's' men had shouted contemptuously at the French soldiers from their tanks: **"Drop your rifles and get the hell out of here – we don't have time to take you prisoners"**[28] **Rommel was well aware that his statement on the terror inflicted on civilians and French troops including the contemptuous orders "**…we don't have time to take you prisoners" by his men could have been presented at Nuremberg **and therefore another reason to escape from Germany.**

l. On June 5, 1940, at Somme, while news of stubborn French resistance was reaching General Von Bock's[29] headquarters, Rommel's 7th Panzer Division had been instrumental in the capture of more than 40,000 prisoners including 12 Generals on 12th June 1940. **Rommel would have had to answer for his action at the Nuremburg Trial and had a reason not to return to Germany after his escape.**

m. In September 1942, when Rommel tried to tell Hitler that he simply did not have the necessary resources to advance to Egypt, Hitler ordered him to go on sick leave in the mountains of the Simmering below Vienna[31]. Rommel did do this to receive a cure for an infected nose and a swollen liver.[32] He would have been aware that his advice would not have gone down well with Hitler. **He would therefore have had a reason for escaping from Germany, particularly when he had lost the Battle of El Alamein.**

n. Early in 1944, Rommel had made himself available to the conspirators to assassinate Hitler. However, his entrance into the plot against Hitler was not approved by most of the resistance leaders who regarded the 'Desert Fox' as a Nazi and as an opportunist who had blatantly courted Hitler's favor and was only now deserting him because he knew the war was lost.[33] Rommel's commitment to aid the conspirators would have included him on Gestapo's list of executions. **He therefore had a reason to fake his own death and escape from Germany.**

o. In January 1944, when Rommel became Commander of Army Group B in the West, the main force with which the expected Anglo-American invasion across the channel was to be repelled, he began to see a great deal of two old friends, General Falkhausen34, and General Stuelpnagel[24] both who had already joined the anti-Hitler conspiracy and gradually initiated Rommel into it. They were aided by an old friend of Rommel, Dr. Karl Stroelin.[50] Towards the end of February 1944, Dr. Stroelin met Rommel at his home at Herrlingen , near Ulm, and had a heart to heart talk in which Rommel declared, "I believe, it is my duty to come to the rescue of Germany".[35] It is worth noting that at this meeting and all subsequent ones which Rommel had with the plotters, he opposed assassinating Hitler – not on moral but on practical grounds. To kill the dictator, he argued, would be to make a martyr of him. He insisted that Hitler be arrested by the Army and haled before a German court for crimes against his own people and those of occupied lands.

On April 15, 1944 General Hans Speidel[36] became Rommel's Chief of staff. He lost no time in going to work on his chief. Within a month, on May 15, he arranged a meeting at a country house near Paris between Rommel, Stuelpnagel and their Chief of staff. The purpose, said Speidel, was to work out **"the necessary measures for ending the war in the west and overthrowing the Nazi regime."[37]**

The above meetings are a clear indication that Rommel would have been implicated in the plot, even though he did not advocate killing Hitler. Nevertheless, he would have still been on Hitler's list of executions, rightly or wrongly and therefore had a reason to escape from Germany.

p. As early as 1942, Von Rundsted[21] knew about the Resistance movement against Hitler among the high-ranking officers of the armed forces, but although he was never a convinced Nazi, he refused to commit himself to the conspiracy. He informed Rommel: "**you are young and you are popular with the people. You must do it.**" That was as far as Von Rundstedt would go in the conspiracy. After the unsuccessful July plot of 1944, Von Rundstedt followed his oath of allegiance to Hitler and presided over the military court of honour that found the conspirators guilty and expelled them from the armed forces prior to their appearances before the People's Court.[25]

Although it was Von Rundstedt who had himself informed Rommel to "do it" (i.e lead the plot to assassinate Hitler), on account of the July plot being unsuccessful, **Rommel would have feared being found guilty by the People's Court presided over by the very Von Rundstedt and therefore would have considered escaping from Germany… the Desert Fox was playing a dangerous Cat and Mouse game with Hitler and those who were die hard Nazis.**

q. Under Hitler's orders, the Gestapo had made a list of 7000 arrests of conspirators to be tried and executed by the People's Court. Then came the time of General Stulpnagel[24] who under torture blurted out Rommel's name followed by Colonel Hofacker[38] who broke down and told of Rommel's part in the conspiracy. "**Tell the people in Berlin they can now count on me,**" Hofacker quoted Rommel as assuring him. It was a phrase that struck in Hitler's mind when he heard of it and which led him to decide that his favorite General, whom he knew to be the most popular one in Germany, must die. **This would have been the most important reason for Rommel to have faked his death and to have escaped from Germany.**

r. Going earlier, on July 13, 1934, in a speech, Hitler wowed to quash all dissent: "**Everyone must know for all future time that if he raises his hand to strike the state, then certain death is his lot.**"[46]

Rommel would have been aware of this all through the war and had a reason to escape from Germany.

s. When Hitler ordered a state funeral for Rommel, Field Marshal Von Rundstedt[21] delivered the funeral oration. "**His heart**" said Rundstedt as he stood over Rommel's swastika-bedecked body, "**belonged to the Fuehrer**".[47] **It is important to note that Rundstedt had stood over Rommel's "swastika – bedecked body." This means that his body was not exposed for anybody to see at the state funeral. Also, after the state funeral, the "body" would have been taken to a crematorium where the ashes would have been put into an Urn ready for burial in his grave.**

In our opinion, through the "pre-arrangements" Rommel had made with his contacts in Berlin, the "body" could have either been of some other dead person or a dummy and the "ashes" in the URN could have been somebody else's collected from the crematorium or simply a handful of sand.

At this juncture, we still have to solve the pending issue of cremation. Assuming that Rommel's corpse was first taken to the hospital (where Burgdorf had warned the pathologist not to touch it) it would have had to be stored in a mortuary. We need to establish the time (hours) it was stored in the "cold room". It was then paraded in a coffin be-decked with a swastika cloth. After the Military honours parade concluded (we need to establish the day and hours it took for this ceremony), the coffin would have had to be taken to a crematorium in the vicinity of the hospital (we need to identify this creamatorium's location and how long the corpse took in an incinerator before the ashes were ready for collection in an Urn. On what day did those responsible collected the Urn and presented it to Rommel's wife/son to place in his grave (or sprinkle the ashes in it)?

t. Desmond Young in his book "Rommel – The Dessert Fox" (pp.251 – 52) wrote: **"It is only fair to add that Rundstedt probably did not know of the circumstances of Rommel's death,** apparently learning them only from Keitel's48 testimony at Nuremburg. "I did not hear these rumours," Rundstedt testified on the stand, "otherwise I would have refused to act as a representative of the Fuehrer at the state funeral that would have been an infamy beyond words." Rundstedt never attended Rommel's cremation after the funeral ceremony.

Here again, since Rundstedt was never brought to the trial and held an important command at NATO in the late 1950's, his testimony "I did not hear these rumours" pertaining to the circumstances of Rommel's death is significant in that Rommel's death itself was in question and not investigated. All this points to Rommel's death and cremation being faked.

u. As recorded in Manfred's Deposition59 dated 29 April, 1945, Rommel had told him that he had been suspected of complicity in the 20th July 1944 Plot to assassinate Hitler and on account of his name appearing as Prime Minister in Goer Delle's list would have, (and did) encountered Hitler's wrath and therefore had a reason to escape from Germany.

v. When he arrived in German Namibia as a civilian by the name of Meyer in c. Oct/Nov 1944 he was only 53 years old. He would have found himself in a state of profound physical and moral depression. His conscious must have haunted him and he sought some redemption from being associated with Hitler's brutal regime and the horrendous atrocities it had carried out on the Jews and others.

A reason for him never to return back to Germany.

w. Although perhaps too late in the day, he would have had a change of heart and felt remorseful for his role as a Commander of the battles in the West, where under his orders, thousands of soldiers and particularly innocent men, women and children had perished.

Another reason for him never to return back to Germany.

x. He certainly was NOT a cold-blooded killer like Himmler, Mengele, Eichman, Borman, Theodore Eicke, Heydrich, Daluege, Heinrich Muller, Franz Huber, Arthur Nebe, Carl Hermann, Manfred Roeder, Bad Tolz, Sepp Dietrich, Fritz Knochlein, Goebbels and other Nazis who executed civilians in occupied territories and millions in the concentrated camps. **The British did NOT hate him but had a grudging admiration of him.** After all, British and American Intelligence were aware of his Anti-Hitler sentiments and in an odd way, considered him to have been a possible ally. Regardless of this, Rommel would have still feared imprisonment at Nuremburg Trial and decided not to return back to Germany.

In concluding here, the above records, in one way or other were more than sufficient reasons for ROMMEL to have had his cremation faked and to have escaped from Germany.

CONCLUSION

We are of the considered opinion that the following ultimately happened:

He had pre-arranged his escape from Germany under the false name of MEYER long before 14th October 1944 for the reasons provided above.

He was secretly informed by General Speidel of Hitler's offer of the choices of either "taking poison" or "stand trial for treason" on 4th September 1944. He therefore had 6 clear weeks to have then pre-arranged his faked death with the assistance of General Burgdorf.

The following chapters now provide compelling evidences recorded from interviews and correspondences with reliable persons that Rommel did NOT take poison, but escaped out of Germany under the false name of MEYER on the days after 14th October 1944 and eventually settled and died in Malawi leaving behind a family.

AUTHORS' COMMENTS

In history we are not allowed to accept evidence without first scrutinizing its substance and origin, regardless of how reputable and scientific our source may be: be it research presented by a University Professor or a lay author. In historiography, we weigh, rather than count or balance our evidence. Scholars, Historians and readers are requested to assess the compelling evidences now provided with an open mind and weigh rather than count the same.

CHAPTER TWO

The Falsified Death Certificate Controversy

INTRODUCTION

According to a news article published in Vox Popoli (18 Nov, 2013), a certain Dr. Friedrich Breiderhoff had made a seven page report to Cologne Police on 22nd July 1960 in which he claimed that he was forced by an S.S. man to falsify Rommel's death certificate by inserting '**Death as a result of a heart attack suffered while in service of the Reich in the war**'. The following are excerpts from the police report based on the Doctor's testimony (as reported in Vox Popoli) which we will examine and provide our arguments to disprove the authencity of his claims:

Dr. Breiderhoff stated, "**It was Herr Rommel. His hat and his marshal's baton were lying to the right of his upper body on the floor.** Then a man in civilian dress appeared and ordered me to begin resuscitation attempts and told me that I must not tell the staff that he was dead. I made a direct cardiac injection with heart massage and breathing exercises, as if the Field Marshal had drowned. I felt completely that Rommel was a dead man already. Then a S.S. man ordered me to remove the vomit from his mouth and I found an empty cyanide capsule in his throat covered with brown and yellow mucus. **I was then ordered that I had to put 'heart attack' on the death certificate on the express orders of the High Command of the Armed**

Forces. An S.S. man told me to maintain confidentiality otherwise I must expect revenge against my family and other consequences. He pointed to a gun laying on a table as if to emphasize the point.

In our opinion, it is doubtful that the S.S. man would have laid a gun on the table, more likely a revolver. Also, when the doctor was summoned to the car to inspect the body where he carried out what he claimed, when and who brought the table from the hospital and placed it next to the car? Moreover, if this did happen, then there was bound to be a member of staff who carried the table to the car and even though he would have been ordered to go back into the hospital, he would have questioned or queried what happened outside the hospital with the doctor or other members of staff.

The news article also states that Rommel's death certificate shows that the Field Marshal succumbed to **"death as a result of a heart attack suffered while in service of the Reich in the west"**.

Our methodical examination of the above statements to disprove Dr. Briederhoff's testimony are presented as follows:

To start off with, the news article stated that Dr. Briederhoff was brought from his post at the **reserve military hospital** at Ulm where he was the chief physician.

Official records and our plausible reconstruction of events state that Rommel's body was taken to the **General Hospital Wagnerschule** on 14th October 1944 by General Burgdoff in another car driven by a civilian driver in S.S. uniform or even another S.S. driver, since the S.S. driver (S.S. Master Sergeant Heinrich Doose) who had driven Burgdoff, Maisel and Rommel to the suicide spot was instructed to drive back Maisel to General Hospital Wagnerschule and wait there.

When Burgdoff took "the body" to this hospital the doctor/pathologist was forbidden to touch the corpse and was told that "everything has been arranged in Berlin".

If Dr. Breiderhoff was telling the truth, why then was there a need for Burgdoff to lie about taking "the corpse" to General Hospital Wagnerschule?

Here again, we don't know where the car containing the 2 senior army officers was parked neither do we know their names.

Dr. Briederhoff, when examining Rommel's body would have noticed that he was in his full military uniform and carried a revolver which he clearly did not report. **(see chapter 4 and 5 regarding Rommel's military uniform and revolver).**

Furthermore, we shall now examine the sequence of "treatment" as administered by Dr. Breiderhoff. He started by saying that a man in civilian dress appeared and ordered him to begin resuscitation attempts. He then stated, "I made a direct cardiac injection and then attempts at resuscitation with heart massage and breathing exercises, as if the Field Marshal had drowned".

In our considered opinion, since the Doctor was summoned from a reserve military hospital to inspect a body in a car outside the hospital by two senior army officers, he could'nt have known as to what to do to the body for him to have carried a cardiac injection in advance.

It is also pertinent to note that he claimed that he conducted breathing exercises "as if the Field Marshall had drowned". **This means that the doctor performed mouth to mouth resuscitation on the body as one would perform on a person who had been rescued from drowning.** The doctor then, as ordered by an S.S. man, removed the vomit from Rommel's mouth (which he would have done) and found an empty cyanide capsule in his throat covered with brown and yellow mucus. Here again, the above does not make sense in that while performing a mouth to mouth resuscitation on Rommel, the doctor would have noticed the vomit covered with brown and yellow mucus or even when he conducted massaging and pressing his heart, the vomit would have spilled out from his throat into his mouth.

From the above inconsistencies, it is clear that the doctor fabricated the whole issue leading to finding an empty cyanide capsule.

We now come to the most important point regarding the whole issue of Dr. Briederhoff's testimony.

The doctor made a seven page report to Cologne Police on July 22, 1960. Even though the doctor was warned not to disclose what had happened in October 14, 1944, he made this report some 15 years and 9 months after what he claimed had happened.

The 2nd World War was over in 1945 and neither did Hitler nor the S.S. exist for the doctor to have feared any revenge on him or his family. On the contrary, he could have even attended the Nuremburg Trial which was held from Nov. 1945 to October 1946 and testified against the two senior army officers and S.S. man who had ordered him to write the wrong cause of death in Rommel's death certificate. **It simply does not make sense for him to have waited this long to have made his report to Cologne Police.**

We now come to the crux of the matter. The doctor claimed that he was forced by an S.S. man to lie on Rommel's death certificate by inserting the cause of death being heart attack following an allied strafing of his car.

We know from official records that 15 minutes after Rommel was taken away from his house in Herlingen on 14th October 1944, a telephone call from the chief doctor at the hospital (General Hospital Wagnerschule and not a reserve military hospital at Ulm) to Frau Rommel in which she was informed that the two generals has brought in the body of the Field Marshal, who had died of cerebral apoplexy (apparently) as a result of his previous skull fractures (which happened on 17th July 1944 after the Allied invasion of Normandy when he was severely injured when his automobile was strafed by a British plane and he was sent home to Ulm to recover).

Now, first of all, the accident happened 3 months prior to the date Frau Rommel received the call and she of course knew that Rommel had recovered but had informed her of what was in store for him.

In our opinion, it made no significant change as to the cause of death in that it makes no sense as to why the doctor had to falsify Rommel's death when in fact, the previous official reasoning was actually more convincing and appropriate.

Furthermore, the article states that "He (Rommel) was honoured at his burial as `Fuehrer's General'. There is an ambiguity in stating 'burial' since Rommel (ie his body) was **NOT buried but cremated** according to official records.

In concluding, in our opinion, Dr. Brierderhoff's testimony does not provide any logical reasons to give weight to its authenticity and therefore is being discarded as "pointless, misleading and totally fabricated".

CHAPTER THREE

First Event Linking to Rommel

BACKGROUND

My nephews' house is located next to mine at Mapanga, 15 kilometers from Blantyre in Malawi. On the night of 26th January 1998, a gang of 5 robbers armed with a AK47 assault rifle and knives broke in the house, shot my elder nephew Mahesh in his lung and stomach and fled after I had returned fire from a shotgun I still own. Mahesh survived after a six month treatment in South Africa. My younger nephew Kamlesh's throat was slit and he died in my arms. We were looking forward to celebrating his first wedding anniversary in six days' time. As head of family, I advertised a reward for the arrest and conviction of the murderers in the local newspaper.

After about one week, a 'coloured'* lady aged about 40 years approached me in my office which is housed in the compound where our furniture factory is located and informed that she had read the reward advert and offered her services to investigate the murder, claiming that she had conducted private investigations on murder cases for senior government officers and asked for a deposit.

I informed her that the reward money of MK 100,000 would only be paid upon her successfully identifying the murderers leading to their arrests and conviction, regardless of whatever method of investigation she would carry out.

She didn't seem happy about my reply and just before she was walking out of my office, I asked her name. She first said "Agrina". I asked "Agrina who?" She said "well actually, Patricia Rommel".

I immediately questioned her, **"You mean THE Rommel?"** she replied, "yes, ofcourse" and left. I didn't believe her and never saw her again.

Dr. Tony Patel
Author

REWARD
K100,000.00
CASH

On Monday, 26th January, 1998, between 9pm & 10pm, about
5 ARMED ROBBERS with guns and knives MURDERED

Mr KAMLESH PATEL and seriously injured
Mr. MAHESH PATEL at their Residence in MAPANGA at Mapanga
Bed & Furniture /Sweet Factory. A CASH REWARD OF K100,000.00
WILL BE GIVEN TO ANY PERSON FOR THE ARREST
AND CONVICTION OF KAMLESH'S MURDERERS.

PLEASE REPORT TO ANY NEAREST
POLICE STATION

16th Nov 1970-26th Jan 1998

2 MALAWI NEWS JAN. 31– FEB. 6 1998 HOME NEWS

4 picked over Mapanga killing

Kamlesh Patel, 27, a student on vacation from the United Kingdom, was part of the family furniture business empire at Mapanga.

He died of panga slashings while his elder brother Mahesh Patel, 33, is in hospital nursing wounds after he was shot in the chest by the armed men.

The gun men killed Kamlesh outside the Patel's Mapanga house when he came out to assist his elder brother who was being butchered by the highwaymen, after they had trailed him as he was driving home from Blantyre in the night.

They caught up with Hamesh inside his courtyard, where confrontation ensued.

Limbe Police confirmed the men were nabbed on Thursday night but refused to disclose details referring repeaters to Police Public Relations Officer Oliver ... claiming it could interfere with investigations.

But police sources at Limbe said the arrest of the suspects was a result of the attractive and bountiful K100,000 cash offer by the concerned and worried-about-crime Indian community.

The cash was to go to anyone with information leading to the arrest of the pitiless murderers.

Somehow, the disgusted Asians heard of the fortunate arrest of the four men the same night police got them; after about 30 of them were told of the apparently breaking news, they assembled and made what they thought was the wise decision of besieging the police station, wanting to 'deal' with the suspects.

Sort out

"...yet, they (Asians) came here at midnight, asking that we should release those boys to them for a few hours."

"They claimed they wanted to 'just sort out a few things' who confessed:

"The situation was so tense they wanted these suspects at all costs."

Police could not give the names of the suspects, saying the matter was still being investigated, nor did they mention the names of the people who gave them information that led to the arrest of the suspects.

Capable

"Are you (reporters) saying we arrested these because someone informed us? We are capable of investigating these cases by ourselves. We need the assistance of the public though," said a proud officer at Limbe, clutching a gun to the police yard.

Full cells

A Malawi News team which sneaked into the police cells noted that they were a lot of suspects.

"We have had a sudden increase in crime in Limbe in recent weeks. That explains why this place is full," added ...

The name Patricia is consistent with the name recorded by Rose Argente in chapter 5 as being one of the twins of Rommel.

*"Coloured". In Malawi and neighbouring countries like Zambia, Zimbabwe and South Africa, the term "coloured" applied and still applies (totally wrongly ofcourse) to children of mixed marriages, e.g. Europeans or Indians marrying local 'black' women.

CHAPTER FOUR

———•———

Second Event Linking to Rommel

INTERVIEW BY DR. TONY PATEL

BACKGROUND

After the murder of my nephew Kamlesh on 26th January 1998, sometime in March, 2002, I had visited the Indian Sports Club in Limbe, Malawi and overheard a conversation on Rommel between Kamal Ganji, a friend, and a Malawian guest. Having remembered the lady who had claimed to be **PATRICIA ROMMEL** (Chapter Three), I made it a point to be introduced to this Malawian guest, who turned out to be a retired Major in the Malawi Army. I invited the Major to my mini museum and he arrived a few days later on a weekend where I interviewed him. Unfortunately, I had mislaid the interview notes and upon recently contacting Kamal Ganji, I was informed that the Major had long since died and both him and I had forgotten his name.

Anyhow, from my recollections of the interview, the Major did mention the following:

a.   That he and another Major used to visit Rommel who stayed with his wife and two children in a caravan parked on a plot just before entering Zomba.

b.   That Rommel had blonde hair and piercing (blue/green?) eyes. That he had attended Rommel's funeral together with the other Major and that there were two other German nationals at his grave during burial.

c. That Rommel had shown both the Majors his General Field Marshal's uniform, revolver and medals including photos taken with Hitler and other photos.

d. That he called himself Meyer and used to drink with them both at Zomba Airfield officer's mess and at Zomba Gymkhana Club.

e. That Rommel appeared to have had plastic surgery done to his nose.

f. That his grave is located in the compound of a house (in which Patricia and Patrick resided) just "behind" Chancellor College in Zomba. He also mentioned that they were like recluses and only visited P.T.C. superette for groceries when these ran out. Unfortunately, I was unable to arrange for the Major to drive me to the grave which he had offered to take me to. Some 15 years later, Rommel's secret family graves were located exactly where the late Major had indicated (it was) they were. See Chapter Twelve.

DEDUCTIONS

1. The Major mentioned of a **CARAVAN** in which Rommel lived which ties up with the one mentioned in Chapter six and seven.
2. He also mentioned of the **TWO CHILDREN** whom both him and the other Major saw at the caravan.
3. The two children, we now know as a certainty were Rommel's twins **PATRICIA & PATRICK** (both mentioned in Chapter five).

4. The Major mentioned Zomba Gymkhana club as one of the clubs which Rommel frequented. This ties up with what Rudolf Hartwich mentioned in chapter Six.

5. The Major mentioned of Rommel calling himself Meyer. This ties up with what is recorded in Chapter Five.

6. The mention of plastic surgery on his nose could have been done in c.1946 in Jo'burg when he was 55 years old.

CHAPTER FIVE

Third Event Linking
to Rommel

BACKGROUND

Dr. Tony Patel, having recalled meeting with Rose Argente beginning of 2015 at his mini museum and mentioning of her having known Rommel alias Meyer, sent her an email on 13th January 2016 requesting details. Rose replied the very same day. Attached are copies of the actual email correspondences between the two. Dr. Patel also requested her bio data which is presented below:

Name:	Rose Argente
Date of Birth:	9th January 1930
Professional Qualifications:	Barrister-at-Law, Lincolns Inn, London, 2001. (Qualified Aged 71 years)

Rose Aged 19 Years   Rose Aged 5o Years

Rose Aged 22 Years
with daughter Lorna
in 1952 when her
father and she knew
Rommel alias Meyer

Rose Aged 86 Years   Rose Aged 86 Years

1. This is the most compelling and credible information on Rommel coming from a Barrister.
2. Rose stated that "he was philosophical and his claim to 'Rommel' was made to my father in confidence — he was a frequent visitor to my parents' home".
3. Rose mentions "I was then at Chirimba when I met Meyer in my parents' home. I believe he came to Chirimba in c. 1953".
4. (Rose would have been 23 years old).
5. "The name 'Rommel' was never used".
6. In the letter dated 6th July 2015 to BBC Audience Service, Rose mentions of "a German named Meyer, a neighbor near my parents' home in Blantyre, Malawi, around 1954-1960". [Rommel would have been 69 years old].
7. Rose also stated "**Meyer claimed to be Rommel and I saw a picture of him in German Uniform**", "He married Grace, a local woman, and they had twins PATRICK and PATRICIA,", "Meyer died in Malawi and was buried at a grave in Zomba (former capital of Malawi)".
8. Most importantly, the evidence provided by Rose more or less ties up with interviews and evidences provided in Chapter Four, Six, and Seven.

Info on Rommel

2 messages

Wed. Jan 13, 2016 at 9:17 AM

To:

Dear Rose,

Please download the attachment

Best Regards Dr. N.D. Patel

Dear Rose,

Further to your visit to my mini museum around January 2014 you had mentioned that you and your late father knew Rommel. Can you please kindly provide the following information:

1. In which year and where did you meet him?
2. How old would he have been?
3. You mentioned he had a daughter and son
4. Was the daughter's name Agrina or Patricia?
5. Was Rommel and his family staying in a caravan near Zomba?
6. When did he die?
7. Where is he buried?
8. In which year did he come to Malawi?
9. Did he come from Namibia?
10. What was his wife's name?
11. Was she a local black woman from Namibia?
12. What did Rommel look like in color of eyes, hair, height?)
13. What did he talk about when he visited your late father?
14. Would you have a photo of him?
15. Would you have any letters/memos written by him to your family member?
16. Any other information which you may recall?

I need the above for a book I am writing on Rommel. Can you also provide your photo and bio details including date and place where you qualified as a Barrister.

Best regards
Dr. Tony Patel (son of D.M. Patel)
Malawi

25/01/2016

Wed, Jan 13. 2016 at 2:11 PM
To:

Dear Tony

So good to hear from you! On Rommel alias Meyer:

1. I was then at Chirimba (before I bought land at Mapanga and built my residence in 1963) when I met Meyer in my parents' home.

    He was a frequent visitor. He and my father were good friends. I believe he came to Chirimba in c.1953and rented a house across the Blantyre/Chileka Road from my father's garage (now the Chirimba Industrial Site).

2. Meyer would then be over 60.
3. See my letter of 06/07/13 to BBC (attached).
4. The name 'Rommel' was never used.
5. When Meyer moved from Chirimba we lost touch.
6. Do not know.
7. See letter to BBC.
8. Meyer may have first come to some other part of Nyasaland. His wife Grace was from Fort Manning (don't know if this British name of a former DC or Governor Manning may have been changed by the new regime of Malawi).
9. Possibly. I do not know.

10. Grace – she was African of the Chipeta tribe.
11. No. See 8 above.
12. Meyer was a grey-haired bent (he may have been 5' 6-7" when younger) old man – possibly 30-40 years older than Grace. I do not recall the colour of his eyes. He gave me the impression he may have been in Nyasaland long enough to know the chichewa words he spoke.
13. **He was philosophical and his claim to 'Rommel' was made to my father in confidence – he was a frequent visitor to my parents' home.**
14. No.
15. None.
16. I brought this matter up with David Stuart-Mogg (he is Co-Editor of Society of Malawi Journal) but he assured me that Rommel was buried in Germany – I have my doubts (See letter to BBC. which I sent while living in Bolton, I now live in Scotland).

My birth date is January 09, 1930. I was called to the Bar of England and Wales at the Honourable Society of Lincoln Inn, London, in 2001 (at age 71).

You may wish to tell me why you need the bio info of me. In the meantime I shall find a photo and send to you with any other info I may have.

Kind regards.

Rose

06 July 2013
BBC Audience Service
P 0 Box 1922
DARLINGTON
DL3 OUR

Dear Audience Service
FIELD MARSHALL ERWIN ROMMEL alias MEYER

I am uncertain as to where I should send this letter but I trust that if your department is not the one to handle this you may wish to send it to the right department. Thank you.

I have a great interest in history and, in fact. I have written a number of historical books. I recently watched the movie The Desert Fox (starring James Mason) about Field Marshall Erwin Rommel (15/11/ 189114/10/1944) which brought back memories of a German named Meyer, a neighbour near my parents' home in Blantyre, Malawi. Around 1954-1960. **Meyer claimed to be Rommel and I saw a picture of him in German uniform.** He married Grace, a local woman, and they had twins, Patrick and Patricia. Meyer died in Malawi and was buried at a Cemetery at Zomba (former capital of Malawi).

w was dubious. It would be interesting to know whether in fact the man buried at a grave at Zomba who posed as Meyer to conceal his identity according to himself, is indeed Rommel.

I was dubious about Meyer's claim at the time. However, many years later a local historian followed the story of Meyer and he was of the opinion from the information he gathered, that the man buried at a grave in Zomba named Meyer was Rommel. Is this something BBC could be interested in? I would appreciate a response.

Kind regards
Rosemary Argente
ROMMEL ALIAS MEYER

Tue, Mar 22, 2016
at 10:28 PM

I managed to find someone who was able to read the notes which you sent when I was unable to read your handwriting. This is an attempt to answer your questions.

Meyer's House
Was on the left side as you go towards Chileka and almost dead opposite my father's garage.

How far down from the Railway line
After the Railway line, about 2,000 yards one comes to the Chirimba bridge then for a few yards, the road inclines slightly upwards, at the top of the incline was the Glen Bar on the left side and Meyer's house was behind the Bar.

You mention Patrick Meyer having a Lodge at Newlands that is almost certainly one of his twin children, the other Patricia.

I have met Deidre Livingstone (Granddaughter of Jervis Livingstone) some years ago in England.

By separate email I have sent you my Dad's bio details and my photo taken yesterday.

I believe this covers all the things you have so far requested. Please let me know if you need anything else.

Kind regards
Rose

Introduction

Although partially relevant, below is presented copy of her certificate having qualified as a Barrister at an age of 71 years, which in itself is a remarkable achievement at this age and in a way, was also an inspiration for my obtaining a PhD in History at the age of 57 years. As evident from her email, she said her father were friends and neighbors of Rommel alias Meyer. Rose, whom I knew way back in 1980, also my neighbor, has written several historical books, a passion which we both share.

Most significantly, her standing as a Barrister lends credibility on her recollections of knowing the very famous Field Marshal who called himself Meyer.

THE HONOURABLE SOCIETY OF LINCOLN'S INN

CERTIFICATE OF STANDING

Rosemary Argente, was admitted into this Honourable Society on the twenty third day of February one thousand nine hundred and ninety, and was Called to the Bar on the eleventh day of October two thousand and one.

In testimony whereof I have hereunto set my hand and the Seal of the Treasurer.

Under Treasurer   Treasurer

ROSE ARGENTE'S RELATIVE IN THE RHODESIAN ARMY – 1944 – IN PREPARATION OF THREAT FROM NEIGHBOURING GERMAN EAST AFRICA

Uncle Robert: Inspection Day by Governor and Army Commander

Uncle Robert: Section 5 March Parade

Uncle Robert: Kit Inspection

CHAPTER SIX

---·---

Fourth Event Linking
To Rommel

BACKGROUND

John Weeks, the co-author, went to Newlands Old Peoples' Home, Off Cholo Road, Limbe in Malawi on Saturday, 16th January 2016 and interviewed a 77 year old German national, who although has slight lapses of memory, provided him with his bio details and the following information on Rommel:

NAME: RUDOLF HARTWICH

Place and Date of Birth: Schneidemuhl, Prussia (Pila in Poland) — 16thFebruary, 1939. Rudolf arrived into Malawi in 1969 aged 30 years and worked as a Electrician. He informed John that he first learnt about Rommel from a book written in German he had read some 15 years ago. From what he read in the book he remembers that

Rommel had bought a caravan in Cape Town, South Africa, had a black woman and frequented a English Club (Zomba Gymkhana Club) in Malawi. He also said that Rommel was buried at Zomba under a different name which was mentioned in this book.

DEDUCTIONS

1. Rudolf read the book in c. 2000 when he was 61 years old.
2. His mention of Rommel purchasing a caravan in Cape Town links up with what John Lord also mentioned in Chapter seven.
3. His mention of the caravan also links up with information provided by the Late Major of Rommel having parked it

on a plot just before entering Zomba (the former capital of British Nyasaland Protectorate) mentioned in Chapter Four.

4. His mention of "having a black woman" ties up with GRACE, the lady Rommel married as mentioned by Rose Argente in Chapter Five.

5. His mention of Rommel being buried at Zomba under a different name ties up with the name MEYER mentioned by Rose Argente in Chapter Five.

6. His mention of Rommel's grave being at Zomba also ties up with the burial ceremony attended by the two Majors mentioned in Chapter Four.

7. The book: At the time of interviewing Rudolf, John Weeks had asked Rudolf if he still had the book. According to John, Rudolf had many books in German language stacked away in his suitcase at his living quarter at the Old People's Home and he was reluctant to let him have the particular book on Rommel. Unfortunately Rudolf passed away at the end of 2016 and his belongings were collected by his estranged wife.

CHAPTER SEVEN

Fifth Event Linking to Rommel

John Weeks, the Co-author happened to phone John Lord, a friend, on 17th January 2016 who was receiving medical treatment in Cape Town, South Africa, basically asking him how he was getting on with the treatment and mentioned in passing about Rommel. John Weeks was astounded to learn from John Lord the following:

He knew of a MEYER who has recently opened a Lodge/Bar across the road where the Old People's Home in which Rudolf Hartwich (mentioned in chapter Six) resides.

Place and Date of birth: Born in Guildford, Surrey UK. On 23rd September 1944.

John qualified as Automotive Engineer and came to Malawi in 1977. His father was a Rocket Scientist at Farnborough. After setting up a Ford factory in Germany, John also set up a similar one in Malawi. He also worked for Tiny Rowland of **LONRHO** and currently retired.

He also mentioned of a caravan which Rommel had purchased in Cape Town, South Africa.

Incidentally this is the very lodge which John Weeks also visited and saw a 'white' person in charge, who served him with drinks.

After learning about what John Weeks heard from John Lord, he drove to the Lodge/Bar on 19th January 2016 to **order a drink and have a chat with the person calling himself MEYER** with a view to finding out whether his first name was **PATRICK**. Upon arrival, the staff informed him that MR. MEYER, the owner had gone to Zambia. John then talked to the Manager and asked for his first name. The Manager said **THUVAN PATRICK!** We now have a living grandson of Rommel alias **MEYER**.

DEDUCTIONS SO FAR

1. John Lord has mentioned of a caravan which is also mentioned in Chapter Four and Chapter Six.
2. Thuvan Meyer is the living grandson of Rommel alias Meyer and now residing in Zambia.

CHAPTER EIGHT

Sixth Event Linking To Rommel

On 10th February, 2016 John Weeks (the co-author) was having a few drinks with his expatriate friends at Mustang Sally Club in Blantyre and had mentioned to them that he was researching about a certain MEYER and his twins Patrick and Patricia.

Another member of the club by the name of MAJID PANJWANI happened to be listening from the adjoining table and matter of factedly mentioned that Patricia was married to his late brother SATTAR. John then arranged for an interview with Majid on 17th February 2016. The following is the information which he obtained.

Brother's name : SATTAR PANJWANI
Date of Birth : 11/6/1948
Date of Death : 9/12/1975
Place of Birth : Chiradzulu, Blantyre
"Married" to Patricia Meyer
Patricia (twin sister of Patrick) born 21/11/1955
Patricia died in c.2008. Buried in family grave. Zomba
Name of daughter : Shamim
Birth date: 19/7/73
Married to Rahim on 1st Jan 1994

Now residing in Jo'burg, South Africa. Children Mariam, Bilal aand Aman

Majid remembered that his late brother Sattar had claimed to be the son-in-law of Rommel. This is the sixth event linking to Rommel.

CHAPTER NINE

Rommel's Legitimate Family in Germany

INTRODUCTION

From historical records[55] it is known that Erwin Rommel married Maria "Lucie" Molllin on 27 November, 1916. Lucie was born at Dirschau (East Prussia) in 1894.

Rommel's grave

Lucie died on 26 December, 1971 at Stuttgart and is buried next to her husband's grave.

Erwin and Lucie had a son by the name of Manfred who was born on 24 December, 1928 at Stuttgart. Manfred married Liselotte Daibar in 1954.

Manfred and Liselotte had daughter by the name of Catherine who was born at on and is still living.

Above left: Manfred
Above middle: Liselotte
Above right: Catherine
Left: Lucie's grave

LUCIA MARIA "LUCIE" MOLLIN ROMMEL

Birth: May 6, 1894, Germany
Death: Sep. 26, 1971
                Stuttgart
                Stuttgarter Stadtkreis
                Baden-Wurttemberg, Germany

Lucie met Erwin Rommel in 1911 while he was attending Officer Cadet School at Danzig West Prussia (Danzig is now part of Poland and is renamed Gdansk). They married on 27 Nov 1916 at Danzig.

Their son Manfred was born in 1928.

Lucie was born at Dirschau (East Prussia) in 1894. She was interested in languages and studied English, French, Latin and other languages at Danzig. Her ancestors came from Italy and Poland.

Lucie died on 26 Dec, 1971 at Stuttgart, Germany and is buried next to her husband Erwin Rommel.

Family links:
    Spouse:
    Erwin Rommel (1891 – 1944)

Children:
    Manfred Rommel (1928 – 2013)*
    *Calculated relationship
    Burial:
    Herrlingen Cemetery
    Blaustein

ROMMEL'S LEGITIMATE FAMILY IN GERMANY

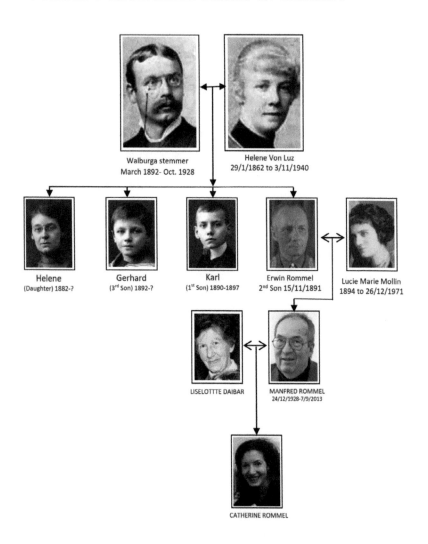

Walburga stemmer
March 1892- Oct. 1928

Helene Von Luz
29/1/1862 to 3/11/1940

Helene
(Daughter) 1882-?

Gerhard
(3rd Son) 1892-?

Karl
(1st Son) 1890-1897

Erwin Rommel
2nd Son 15/11/1891

Lucie Marie Mollin
1894 to 26/12/1971

LISELOTTTE DAIBAR

MANFRED ROMMEL
24/12/1928-7/9/2013

CATHERINE ROMMEL

CHAPTER TEN

Rommel's Secret Family in Germany

INTRODUCTION

In an article titled "Rommel letters reveal secret second family" published in the Sunday Times by Jack Grimston and Michael Wood (July 22, 2001), Erwin Rommel met Walburga Stemmer (March 1892-October 1928) and had an affair with her who gave birth to his daughter, Gertrud Stemmer (later Mrs. Gertrud Pan), on December 8, 1913. Walburga died in 1928, when Rommel's wife Lucie was pregnant with the couple's son Manfred. Her cause of death was given as pneumonia, though it is generally accepted that she probably committed suicide.

Rommel with girlfriend Walburga

Gertrud with son Josef Pan   Rommel with wife Lucie

Erwin's and Walburga's illegitimate daughter Gertrud was born at Weingarten, a town in Wuttenberg, in the District of Ravensburg, Germany. She died in 2000 at the town of Kempton.

She married Joseph Pan, a fruit vendor, and had three children, Joseph, Helga and Anton. Gertrud exchanged hundreds of letters with her famous father. She knitted him a scarf which he wore frequently at the battlefront.

Lucie, wife of Erwin Rommel, knew about Gertrud. Lucie explained to her children that Gertrud was their cousin, when she was actually their older half-sister.

Gertrud was a frequent visitor to the family of Erwin Rommel and was at Rommel's hospital bedside after he returned ill from Africa. There, she answered the telephone when a furious Hitler ordered Rommel back to Africa. She stayed close to the family even after her father's "death".

ROMMEL'S SECRET FAMILY IN GERMANY

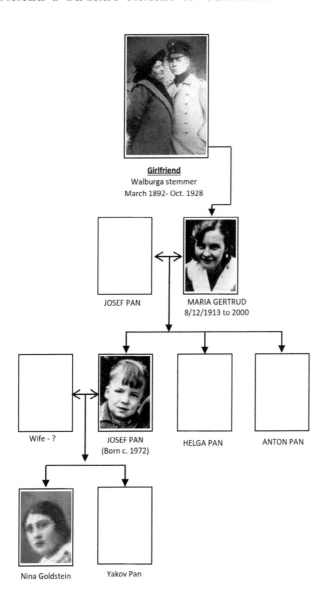

Girlfriend
Walburga stemmer
March 1892- Oct. 1928

JOSEF PAN

MARIA GERTRUD
8/12/1913 to 2000

Wife - ?

JOSEF PAN
(Born c. 1972)

HELGA PAN

ANTON PAN

Nina Goldstein

Yakov Pan

CHAPTER ELEVEN

―――・―――

Rommel's Secret Family in South Africa

INTRODUCTION

When Rommel alias Meyer left Namibia in c.1945, he had arrived in Pretoria in South Africa and befriended Germans. Here he met a Afrikaner lady (about 32 years old) and "married" her. Rommel would have been 54 years old. This union produced two children by the names of Patrick and Patricia. Patrick was born in Johannesburg on 215t March 1946. He married Veronica Ann Verrall (born in Port Elizabeth on 20th March 1943) and they had a son Thuvan (born on 15th November 1966) who married Tiyanjane Amina on 23rd January 2007. Thuvan now resides in Zambia and has 2 children named Kardota Meyer (born on 13th June 2006) and Khylinapthy Meyer (born on 23rd January 2011). Patrick died on 1st March 2001 and is buried alongside Rommel in Zomba, Malawi.

ROMMEL'S SECRET FAMILY IN SOUTH AFRICA

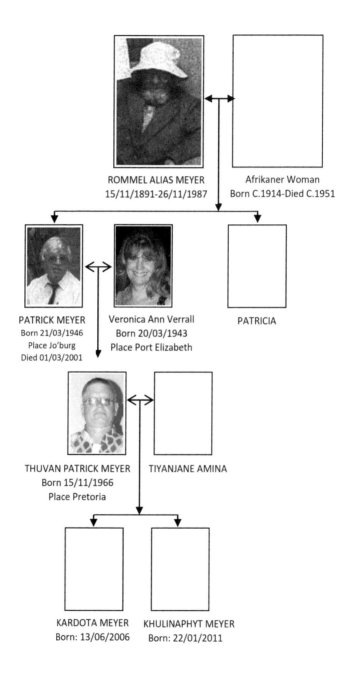

ROMMEL ALIAS MEYER
15/11/1891-26/11/1987

Afrikaner Woman
Born C.1914-Died C.1951

PATRICK MEYER
Born 21/03/1946
Place Jo'burg
Died 01/03/2001

Veronica Ann Verrall
Born 20/03/1943
Place Port Elizabeth

PATRICIA

THUVAN PATRICK MEYER
Born 15/11/1966
Place Pretoria

TIYANJANE AMINA

KARDOTA MEYER
Born: 13/06/2006

KHULINAPHYT MEYER
Born: 22/01/2011

———·———

CHAPTER TWELVE

Rommel's Secret Family in Malawi

SEVENTH EVENT LINKING TO ROMMEL

INTRODUCTION

Referring to records cited in preceding chapters, Rommel alias Meyer had arrived in the British Protectorate of Nyasaland, now Malawi, from South Africa in c. 1949 aged about 58 years and "married" a local woman by the name of Grace (born in c. 1921 and died on 17th September 1992).

He had a son named Patrick (same name given to his other son from his South African partner) and four daughters named Patricia, Hendrina, Violet and Marie. Patrick was born on 21st November 1955 and died on 29th October 1997. He married a Malawian lady by the name of Margaret, born on 28th February 1954. Patrick and Margaret had two sons, a daughter and three grandchildren (see family tree).

Rommel's daughter Patricia (twin sister of Patrick) had first "married" Sattar and had a daughter Shamim (born on 19th July 1973) who married Rahim and has three children, all now living in Jo'burg, South Africa.

When the Author corresponded with Shamim on 3rd April 2017, she informed him that her aunt Hendrina had told her about her grandfather being ROMMEL. This is the Seventh event linking to Rommel who died on 26th November 1987 aged 96 years. See photos of family graves (all buried in Malawi).

ROMMEL'S SECRET FAMILY IN MALAWI

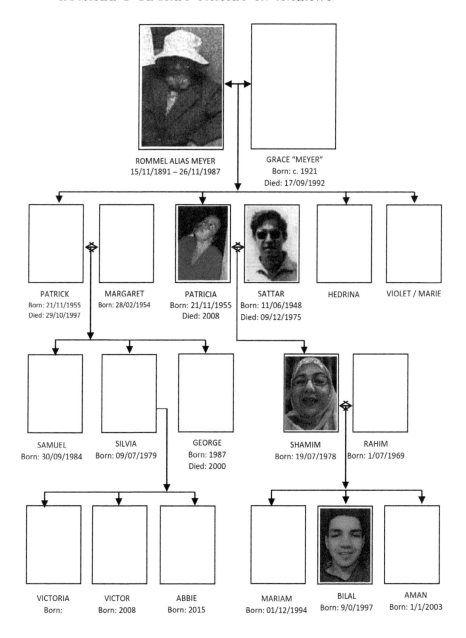

ROMMEL ALIAS MEYER
15/11/1891 – 26/11/1987

GRACE "MEYER"
Born: c. 1921
Died: 17/09/1992

PATRICK
Born: 21/11/1955
Died: 29/10/1997

MARGARET
Born: 28/02/1954

PATRICIA
Born: 21/11/1955
Died: 2008

SATTAR
Born: 11/06/1948
Died: 09/12/1975

HEDRINA

VIOLET / MARIE

SAMUEL
Born: 30/09/1984

SILVIA
Born: 09/07/1979

GEORGE
Born: 1987
Died: 2000

SHAMIM
Born: 19/07/1978

RAHIM
Born: 1/07/1969

VICTORIA
Born:

VICTOR
Born: 2008

ABBIE
Born: 2015

MARIAM
Born: 01/12/1994

BILAL
Born: 9/0/1997

AMAN
Born: 1/1/2003

Introduction

Below are photograph of the unmarked grave of Rommel alias Meyer alongside grave of some of his secret family members buried in a private cemetery in Zomba, Malawi. Information on the cemetry's location and names of buried family members was provided by Shamim, grand-daughter of Rommel, living in Johannesburg, South Africa.

Rommel Alias Meyer 15/11/1891 – 30/11/1987

Patrick (S. Africa) 21/3/1946 – 1/3/2001

Patrick (Malawi) 21/11/1955 – 29/10/1997

Hendrina

Patrik (S. Africa) 21/3/1946 – 1/3/2001

As would be expected, although slightly inconsistent in dates and places, various evidences have been provided by us in this book pointing to Rommel's final resting place being that in Malawi and not in Germany, the most credible and compelling being the one that is provided by Rose Argente, Barrister-at-Law.

For the sake of History, we are requesting that both the British and German Governments (now friends) including universities and the like dealing or interested in research related to Rommel obtain further scientific data to establish whether he died in Germany or in Malawi in the following manner:

1. Whether or not it was "his body" that was cremated in Germany (which we now doubt), DNA* from the ashes would be impossible to obtain.
2. With permission of his grandson Thuvan living in Zambia, DNA from his skeletal remains (eg teeth) from his grave at Zomba be obtained. And although this will not be necessary, it will provide the absolute proof of him being laid to rest in Malawi (and ofcourse all the reasons for his escape from Germany).
3. DNA (saliva swab) from his grandson Thuvan living in Zambia be obtained with his permission.
4. DNA (saliva swab) from his grand-daughter CATHERINE living in Germany be obtained with her permission.
5. DNA (saliva swab) from his grand-daughter Shamim born in Malawi and now living in South Africa be obtained with her permission.
6. Comparison of the DNA results of his living relatives in Germany with those living in Zambia and South Africa.

We are absolutely confident that the above scientific tests, if carried out, will put an end to the controversy over the death and final resting place of Rommel, Germany's most brilliant General Field Marshal, the Desert Fox who was, even in war, grudgingly admired by Field Marshal Bernard Montgomery during the battle at El Alamein in North Africa which the Germans lost on the night of November 2-3, 1942.

Field Marshal Montgomery with HM King George IV-Oct, 1944

Recently, Montgomery paid tribute70 to Rommel in which he said, "I always hoped that one day I might meet Rommel" and "He was a worthy opponent and I always respected him".

Speaking in the House of Commons in 1942, Winston Churchill said of Rommel, "We have a very daring and skillful opponent against us, and may I say across the havoc of war, a great general."

This book is first of its kind which after over 74 years, beckons history to stand to be corrected and to be re-written on the Desert Fox who, in this case, outfoxed Hitler and his tormentors on 14th October, 1944 and escaped from Germany under the false name of MEYER.

Dr. Tony Patel
John Stretton Weeks
Malawi. 2019

*Latest DNA tests which may include (where applicable), autosomal DNA and chromosomal DNA, mitrochondrial DNA and Y chromosomal, Electron Spin Resonance, Mrna, T rna etc

REFERENCES

1. Louis L. Snyder, "*Encyclopedia of the Third Reich*," Wordsworth Editions, Herts ,UK, 1998, p.299.
2. El Alamein : *Ibid*...p.83
3. General field Marschall (GFM, General Field Marshal) The Highest Rank in the German armed forces. In addition to the prestige of an exalted rank, the *General field marschall* received the annual salary of 36,000 reinchsmarks plus allowance, all of it exempt from income tax. Rommel was promoted to the rank by Hitler in 1942.
4. William L. Shirer, " *The Rise and Fall of the Third Reich*," Simon & Schuster, New York , 1960, p.1077
5. Burton Graham, "*Escape from the Nazis,*" Castle Books, NJ, 1975, p.30.
6. William L. Shirer, "*The Rise...*," p.1077.
7. *Ibid*...p.1077.
8. *Ibid*...p.1078.
9. Louis L. Snyder, "*Encyclopedia of...*" p.299.
10. Fredrick V. Grundfeld , "*The Hitler File*," Book Club Associates, London 1974, p.333.
11. *Ibid* ...p.338.
12. *Ibid*...p.339.
13. *Ibid*...p.339.
14. *Ibid*...p.338
15. Robert Wallace et al, "*World War 2,*" Time Life Books inc, Canada, 1979, p.81.
16. Chris Ellis & Peter Chamberlain, "*Fighting Vehicles*," Hamlyn, London,1979, p.59.
17. Kesserling Albert (1885-1960) General Field Marshal in the Luftwaffe. On May 6 1947, a British court martial convicted him on a charge of having allowed the shooting of 335 Italian civilians in reprisal for an attack by Italian partisans on a

German company. He was sentenced to death, but the penalty was commuted to life imprisonment in Oct 1947. He was pardoned and freed in Oct 23, 1952 and died in Bad Nauhelm on July 16, 1960.

18. Robert Wallace et al, *"World War 2,"* p.81.
19. *Ibid* ...p.54.
20. *Ibid*...p.181.
21. Rundstedt, Gerd Von (1875-1953) General field Marshal in the armed forces of the Third Reich and one of its highest – ranking officers. He died in Hannover on Feb 24, 1953
22. Brig. Peter Young, *"World War 2,"* Bison Book, London, 1980, p.194.
23. Beck, Ludwig (1880-1944). Chief of staff of the armed forces from 1935 to 1938 and a central figure in the resistance and conspiracy movements against Hitler.
24. Stulpnagel, Karl Heinrich Von (1886-1944). Military governor of occupied France and principal agent in Paris of the conspiracy against Hitler. A close friend of Rommel whom he tried to persuade to use his influence to end the war in the west before the expected allied invasion. Stulpnagel was hanged in Berlin on Aug 30, 1944.
25. Kluge, Gunther Hans Von (1882-1944). General field Marshall in the armed forces of the third Reich. A non-Nazi, he was by nature indecisive. Although he indicated that he might take part in the conspiracy, he relapsed into complaint obedience to Hitler. He committed suicide on Aug 18, 1944, on a former battlefield of 1870 west of Metz.
26. Brig, Peter Young, *'World War 2,"* p.194.
27. Robert Wernick et al, *"Blitzkrieg,"* Time Life Books, Canada, 1976, p.119
28. *Ibid*...p.120.
29. Robert Wernick et al, *"Blitzkrieg"*, General field Marshall in the armed forces of the Third Reich, killed in an air raid on May 4, 1945.
30. Robert Wernick et al, *"World..."* p.185.
31. William L. Shirer, *"The Rise ... "* p.915.
32. *Ibid* ...p.919.

33. *Ibid...*p.1030.
34. Falkenhausen, Alexander Freiherr Von (1876-1966). General of infantry, Military Governor of Belgium and northern France. Tried by Belgian military tribunal, he was accused of executing hostages and deporting Jews and Belgian workers. On March 9, 1951, he was sentenced to twelve years penal servitude but was soon released. He died in Nassau on July 31, 1966.
35. William l. Shirer, "The Rise...,"p.1031.
36. Speidel, Hans (1897-1987), General in the Wehrmacht and memberof the Resistance movement. In 1955, he represented the West German Republic in the North Atlantic Treaty Organisation. Beginning on Nov 22 1955, he served as chief of the Armed Forces Dept. of the Defense Ministry of the Federal Republic. He died in 1987.
37. William L. Shirer, "*The Rise...,*"p.1032
38. Hofacker, Caeser Von (1896-1944). A member of the officer's conspiracy against Hitler. Was found guilty of treason by the People's Court in Berlin and executed on Dec 20, 1944.
39. William L. Shirer, "*The Rise...*" P.1077.
40. Burgdorf Wlilhem, General in the armed forces of the Third Reich. An alcoholic believed to have shot himself in the cellar of the New Chancellory, May 1945.
41. Maisel Ernest, General in the armed forces of the Third Reich. An alcoholic.
42. Goebbels, Paul Joseph (1897-1945). High ranking National Socialist politician, close friend of Hitler and propaganda expert of the Third Reich. Committed suicide in April, 1945.
43. Model, Walter (1891-1945), General field marshal. Under his command, some 325,000 German troops and thirty generals were captured by the allies. Rather than become a prisoner, Model shot himself in a forest between Dusseldorf and Duisburg and died on April 21, 1945.
44. Hess, Walter Richard Rudolf (1894-19870. Deputy to Hitler and at one time his appointed successor after Herman Goring. Tried at Nuremberg and sentenced to life imprisonment. He died a Spandau prison in 1987.

Enemy Within - First World War

This indenture is dated February 1917 Between William Hill McCullough "The custodian of enemy property for the Nyasaland Protectorate and JOHN TENNET. The property was Seized from HERMANN ENRHARDT who was described as an "ENEMY WITHIN THE ORDINANCE" and John Tennett being the highest bidder, acquired 3000 acres of land in Luchenza for the princely sum of 1200 pounds sterling.

45. Enemy within the ordinance: above is an example of property seized from Herman Enrhardt in British Nyasaland and although this happened during World War 1, the British would have done the same to Germans living in Malawi during World War 2. However in 1950's Meyer alias Rommel would not have been considered an enemy within the ordinance since over 4 Years had elapsed after the war.

46. The editors, *"The SS,"* Time Life Book, Virginia, 1988, p.37.

47. William L. Shirer, *"The Rise...,"* p.1079.

48. Keitel, Wilhelm Bodewine Johan (1882-1946). General field marshal in the armed forces of the third Reich and Hitler's chief Military adviser in World War 2. He was mounted on the gallows in the execution chambers of Nuremburg prison on Oct 16, 1946.

49. Mussolini, Benito Amilcare Andrea (1883-1945). Director of fascist Italy from 1922 to 1943 and ally of Hitler and the Third Reich. Captured by Italian partisans together with other fascist leaders and his mistress, Clara Petacci. All were executed on April 28, 1945.

50. Dr Stoelin Karl: Rommel's civilian friend, who in August 1943 had persuaded him to join in drawing up a memorandum to the Ministry of the Interior – now headed by Himmler – in which they jointly demanded a cessation of the persecution of the Jews and Christian Churches, the restoration of Civil rights and the re-establishment of a system of justice divorce from the party and the S.S. – Gestapo.

51. In 2008, Andreas Rusch, the Author's business contact in Pretoria, had invited him to a dinner at his late father's house where he saw Hitler's portrait and Nazi paraphernalia. The father was in his late 80's and had claimed to have worked under 'Farmers' Co-operative' during the war.

52. Louis L. Snyder, "Encyclopedia…," p.303.

53. Jesse Green span, "Things you may Not know about Erwin Rommel," Google, October 14, 2014.

54. Douglas Martin, "Manfred Rommel, Son of German Field Marshal, Dias at 84," The New York Times, Nov9, 2013.

55. Wikipedia, 2/14/2016.

56. Krebs Hans : Bio-data Mislaid

57. Goering, Hermann Wilhelm (1893-1946) No. 2 Nazi, Hitler's heir apparent, and high military and economic leader of the Third Reich. In 1946 he was brought before the International Military Tribunal at Nuremburg. He was found guilty on various counts and sentenced to death. On October 15, 1946, two hours before he was to be hanged at Nuremberg, Goering took a vial of poison

that somehow had escaped the vigilance of his guards. At the order of the court his ashes were thrown into the last remaining incinerator at Dachau.

58. Editors, *"The Luftwaffe"*, Time-Life Books, Virginia, 1982, p. 170

59. Deposition: Manfred's typed –written account was made on April 27, 1945, when the Allies had all but won the war in Europe, and is believed to have been dictated by him as it is in English. The two-page document has come to light after it was sold at auction as part of an archive of other wartime mementoes.

60. Aldinger, Captain Hermann, *"The Rommel Papers"* , 1953, p. 207-212

61. Ehrenburger Major : Bio-data Mislaid

62. Diels, Rudolf (1900-1957): Ministerial Councillor and first chief of the Gestapo. In June, 1933 Goering appointed Diels chief of Department 1A in the Prussian State of Police, attached to the Ministry of the Interior. This organization eventually became the Gestapo. After the July Plot against Hitler in 1944, he was arrested and put in a Gestapo prison. Having survived the fall of the Third Reich, he was employed as a provincial administrator in Lower Saxony. He died in 1957.

63. Friedrich Huober: From a statement made by Captain Aldinger dated 15th October 1944. Letters were edited by B. H. Liddell Hart and published as *The Rommel papers*

64. William L. Shirer, *"The Rise..."* p. 1078

65. Rommel Letters: Bio-data Mislaid

66. Another example of actual document

67. Mixed Marriage: SPECIAL LICENCE. On the right is copy of licence to intermarry. This was mandatory in British

Nyasaland right up to 1950. Rommel alias Meyer would have had to obtain such a licence if he had married Grace the "black" women.

68. Source of article mislaid.
69. Field marshal Montgonery : Source Mislaid
70. Dinge en Goete : This day in WWII history : Feb 21, 1941 : Rommel in Africa.

RESEARCH MATERIAL

Introduction

Attached are emails sent to (a) Immigration officials of the Namibian Ministry of Home Affairs inquiring if a passenger by the name of MEYER entered Namibia between October and December 1944. Despite sending a reminder, no response was received. Any information on MEYER from their archives would have tied up our reconstruction of the journey made by Rommel under the false name of MEYER and (b) Catherine Rommel, the legitimate grand-daughter of Rommel living in Germany. No response received

Namibia – Ministry of Home Affairs
Date: 3oth June 2017
Subject: INQUIRY

Dear Sir/madam,
I shall be most grateful to you if you would kindly respond to my
email dated 6`'" May 2017.

Kind regards
Dr. Tony Patel

> Directorate: Immigration and Border Control
> Ms. Elizabeth Negumbo
> Job Title. Chief of Immigration

> Department: Border Control
> Mr Nehernia Nghishekwa
> Job Deputy Director

> Department: Citizenships and Passports
> Mr Allison Hishekwa
> Job Title: Deputy Director

> Depan merit Refugee Administration
> Division: Population Services

From:
To:
Cc:
Date: 6 May 2017, 10:31 a.m.
View security details

Dear Madam,
I shall be most grateful if you would Confirm from your immigration archives if a German passenger by the name of Meyer arrived at Windhoek Airport between October 1944 and December 1944. any further information (eg photograph) on this passenger will be most appreciated and will assist towards my research on a book I am writing. A photo of the airport (1944) and type of passenger plane which would have landed at Windhoek from German east Africa will also be helpful

Kindly acknowledge receipt of this email.

warm regards

Date: 30th June 2017
Subject: INQUIRY

Dear Madam,
About a month ago I sent you an email in which 1 inquired if you were Catherine Rommel as per the above email and if so, wanted to contact you re: your late grandfather Field Marshal Erwin Rommel.
    Please respond. Kind regards
    Dr. Tony Patel
    Malawi

Inquiry Add label
Narhari Patel

8:20 a.m. View details

Dear madam,
Would you be Catherine rommel as per the above email address? I would like to contact you regarding your late grandfather general field Marshall Erwin Rommel who escaped Germany in October 1944 and is buried in Malawi. Leaving behind another family.
    Kind regards
    Dr. Tony Patel

HOMAGE

This book has been written in memory of my father, the late Shree Dr. Dayalji Morarji Patel who came to Malawi in 1928 at the age of 21 on his own since his father and elder brother, who were settled in King William's Town in South Africa since 1904, did not wish him to join them there.

He arrived armed only with a City of Guilds Certificate (Birmingham University, issued at Baroda 1926) in land surveying and a gold medal (matriculation, Baroda High School) bestowed on him by none other than Sardar Vallabhai Patel, India's Iron Man and a fellow Leuva Patidar and built his empire through hard work, honesty and generosity.

He first worked for Mr. Hussein Arbi for two years at his shop in the village of Chief Chapananga in the Chikwawa District from where he had to travel a distance of 45 km on foot through jungles to Blantyre every weekend to deliver money from sales to his employer. Within two years, he saved enough money and purchased a plot in Tsapa for seven pounds from Mr. Ismail Mahomed (father-in-law of the prominent Malawi born Barrister Mr. Rashid Osman) and built a shop.

Between 1931 and 1951 he brought all his cousins and their families from India to Malawi and apart from owning the largest

Indian owned parcels of land in the country, he also established the first dairy farm, furniture factory, printing press, soft drinks factory, nail manufacturing enterprise, Cinema, transportation, Garage, and the first Indian owned cotton and tobacco estates on a large scale. At the height of his successful business years he employed over 5000 Malawians and 40 Indian management staff.

He first took a Ford Mercury Saloon Car to India in 1944 which is still operational as a Taxi in Navsari owned by a Muslim gentleman.

Jawaharlal Nehru, India's first Prime Minster toured the State of Gujerat in one of his Chevrolet Bel-Air just after Independence.

He was known as the 'Lion of Chikwawa' by the succession of British District Commissioners in Chikwawa who became his personal friends and subsequently also became a personal friend to all the Governors who were administrating the country during this period including Sir Robert Armitage, Governor of the Federation of Rhodesia and Nyasaland, whose Humber Super snipe official car he purchased.

Dayalji in his Chevrolet 1953

Being one of the prominent leaders of the Hindu community he afforded financial assistance to many members of the Hindu, Muslim, Sikh, Goan and Malawian communities. He sponsored the education in India of the children of the Mungwira family where Mr. Mungwira's son and daughter qualified as chemists and joined the company of Lever Brothers in the late 1960s. He also built the Patel Seva Samaj Hall in Limbe and leased a building to the First President of Malawi Dr. Hastings Kamuzu Banda for use as surgery when he had returned here from his imprisonment at Gwelo prison in the then Southern Rhodesia. The Sikh community honoured him by bestowing on him the title of 'Sardar' in 1944 which was also bestowed upon me in 2002.

Just after partition, it was normal practice for Muslim Shopkeepers in Malawi to obtain donations from their fellow brethren with the approval of the Jamaat (Muslim Council) to construct Mosques in the towns they had settled. There was an incident whereby one certain Muslim Shopkeeper refused to donate towards the construction of a Mosque in the town he had his Shop. Some senior members of the Jamaat actually approached Dayalji and requested him to intervene. He gladly drove with the Jamaat members to this man's shop and upon inquiring as to why he was refusing the small donation of five pounds for a Holy cause, he said to Dayalji in Gujerati, "Uncle Dayalji, here is a cheque for fifty pounds…I am giving it only to you…I can never donate to these thieves (of the Jamaat)", pointing a finger at them. This shopkeeper was a Muslim from Surat. Sadly today, the "Surti" Muslims and the "Mehman" Muslims have built two separate Mosques in Lilongwe, the Capital City of Malawi.

On the morning of India's first Independence Day which was going to be celebrated at the Indian Sports club, a British police officer arrived at the club and removed the Indian flag. Upon learning about this, Dayalji drove up to the office of

Commissioner of Police, put a .22 pistol on the Commissioner's head and demanded that his officer who removed the flag personally hoist it...an order which was promptly followed. When the Commissioner later complained to the Governor, he was instructed to apologise personally to Dayalji. During 2nd World War he had facilitated the storing of British army arsenal in his warehouses in Mangochi and Blantyre, a favour which the Governor and his predecessors had not forgotten. He was later honoured by being the only Indian to be introduced to the Queen Mother at Zomba during her visit to Malawi. (1957 at Governor's Residence, Zomba)

Among the prominent people who stayed with him during their visit to Malawi were Dr. S. Radhakrishna (Philosopher and President of India) and Apasahib Pant, who was India's High Commissioner in Kenya. The latter had even offered him to arrange for the post of Head of Bombay customs, a post he declined to take up.

After spending two years reading the Bible and Quran, he toured various countries in Africa to spread Mahatma Gandhi's message of 'Satyagraha' where the Prime Minister of India, the late Indira Gandhi sent him a letter wishing him success in his mission. He retired as Sarpanch (head of village) in his village of Hari Dhaman in Gujerat where he passed away in 1978. The village people gave him a Samadhi, a fitting tribute to a true patriot and son of India.

PRIME MINISTER

No. 1171-PMO/68

New Delhi
November 13, 1968.

Dear Dr. Patel,

Thank you for your letter. I am glad to learn that, with the blessings of Acharya Vinoba Bhave and Shri Ravishanker Maharaj, you are touring the countries of Africa to popularise Gandhiji's ideas during the centenary year of his birth.

It was on the continent of Africa that Gandhiji perfected the technique of satyagraha. Gandhiji's own life, therefore, is a link between our two great continents which have been partners in suffering and partners in freedom. They can now be partners in the peaceful evolution of humanity.

Wishing you success in your work.

Yours sincerely,

(Indira Gandhi)